Back in the Days of
Prophets and Kings:
Old Testament Homilies
for Children

Jill H. Small

Living the Good News, Inc.
a division of The Morehouse Group
Editorial Offices
600 Grant Street, Suite 400
Denver, CO 80203

Illustrations: Marcy Ramsey, Anne Kosel, Ansgar Holmberg, Betsy Johnson, Victoria Bergesen

Printed in the United States of America.

ISBN 1-889108-18-9

Table of Contents

Introduction

You invite them forward with a mixture of both joy and apprehension, these children of assorted sizes and ages. Adults shift to allow the escape from cramped pews and closely packed chairs. Small forms drop out into the aisles, then bob forward toward the front of the church, some holding hands, some looking back questioningly at parents. Many grin; others share your apprehension. They surround you, watching you closely, waiting for your smile, your touch, your greeting. You know you take a risk each time you welcome this unpredictable group forward, but you also know, as you settle together at the front of the church, that the next few minutes will be among the most rewarding of your week.

Each parish calls it something different: a children's message, perhaps, or a children's sermon or children's talk. Here we refer to it as a children's homily, a short presentation, based on a scripture story, that invites the children to enter into and experience the story of our faith. Each homily respects the children's own spiritual vitality, urging them to share their experience of God, themselves and each other in an environment of love and safety.

Why offer children their own homily?

Offering a children's homily says to the children: "This is a special time just for you, because *church is for you, too.* Here, in church, you are welcomed, delighted in, treasured, held in our arms as you are held in God's arms." A children's homily extends in a concrete way the embrace of our loving God to include these, God's most vulnerable children. "You are this important to us," is the message, as the children file forward to gather for their homily.

But a children's homily offers the children more than the important affirmation that church is their place, too. A well-prepared children's homily couches the basics of Christian experience in terms the children understand and own. It invites children to experience the truths of scripture from the inside out: Children don't learn *about* Jesus calming the storm, they imagine themselves, frightened and rain-soaked, clinging to the sides of the rocking boat, yearning for safety, holding their breath for the moment when Jesus says "Peace, be still," feeling the relief that Jesus brings to the storms they experience in day-to-day life. Children don't learn about the comfort of Jesus' hug, they exchange Jesus' hugs with each other, then take those hugs out into the congregation. You get the idea.

And the benefits of a children's homily go farther than the children themselves. If you regularly present children's homilies, you already know how often adults approach you after the service and say, "That was great. I got more out of your children's homily than the regular homily." A children's homily—perhaps *because* it presents its point so simply and clearly, with the added framework of childlike wonder and innocence—can profoundly impress and move. Never underestimate the power of a child's fresh perspective or sudden and unexpected insight.

Many of the adults watching from the pews don't have children, or have little regular contact with small children. The children's homily helps balance their lives with the wonder and delight the children take in these encounters with God and scripture.

In addition, when you present the children's homilies, you model for families, friends and relatives ways to engage the children they love in the journey of faith. Story-telling, movement, songs, games and the use of props and illustrations—all of these explore faith in simple ways that others can use as well. After a month or two of watching children's homilies, people begin to catch on, even unconsciously adopting the methods demonstrated in your children's homilies.

Who are these homilies for?

Back in the Days of Prophets and Kings: Old Testament Homilies for Children drawn from the second half of the Old Testament contains forty homilies, written for children from the age of four or five through eleven or twelve. Admittedly, this is a broad age range, and you may find some homilies seem more appropriate for the younger children than the older. We have attempted to provide something for all ages in each homily, including occasionally offering options within the homilies themselves. Keep in mind that a children's homily is not an instructional activity, and that age matters less when sharing in ritual and worship. In fact, a variety of responses can enrich the experience for all participants. You may want to invite older children to help younger children with certain tasks and responses. The older children will benefit from the sense of awe and wonder—the raw spirituality —of the younger children.

These homilies will work for both small and large groups, from less than half a dozen to as many as thirty or more. When appropriate, we suggest ways to change the homily for very small or very large groups; for example, in a large group, you may not be able to invite every child to offer a response to every question; do your best to let different children answer each question. In a small group, you may be able to reproduce a simple prop for each child to take home. For the most part, the size of the group will not matter, but if it does, you should be able to adapt each homily for the number of children you anticipate coming forward.

If you regularly have a larger group (more than twelve), consider recruiting another adult or teenage helper for each additional six or so children. This is particularly helpful when the homily includes more complex activities, or if another leader can provide a calming influence for restless children.

How do I prepare?

Each homily in this book includes:
- a scripture reference
- a quote from the reading
- a brief summary of both the reading and the homily
- a materials list
- directions for the homily
- a suggestion for closing prayer

We encourage you to begin your preparation by reading the scripture on which the homily is based. You might consider reading the story in two Bible versions, including *Today's English Version,* used in the preparation of these homilies. Think about the passage. You might ask yourself:
- What does this reading say to me?
- What truth about God, about others or about myself do I learn from this reading?

Then extend your question to include the children you anticipate will join you for the homily:
- What would I like the children to hear in this story?
- What does this reading say to them about the love and care of God?

After your own consideration of the reading, read through the summary of the reading and the homily, check the materials list and read once through the homily itself.

Most homilies in this book offer both an age-appropriate retelling of the scripture story and at least one activity to help the children enter into the meaning of the story (occasionally both story and activity are blended into one overall activity). Time limitations or personal preference may require that you use one or the other rather than both. Feel free to do so. The stories can stand alone; if you

wish, a question or two taken from the activity may be enough to help you draw a story-only homily to a conclusion. Likewise, you may not wish to retell the story if it has just been read from the Bible or lectionary; in this case, simply follow the regular reading of scripture with the homily activity.

Once you decide how much of the homily you wish to present, gather your materials and practice telling the story. We encourage you to memorize the story, though you may certainly use your own words if you wish. Tell the story to yourself, a friend or a family member once or twice. Inexperienced at storytelling? Familiarize yourself with the two cardinal rules of storytelling—make eye contact with your listeners and make sure they can hear you!

At the conclusion of each homily we offer a prayer. Again, add to or adapt each prayer as you wish.

Some basic principles to keep in mind:
- *The younger the children, the shorter the homily.* One guideline suggests that children will sit still and listen one minute for each year of their age; for example, the average five-year-old will be there, attending to you, for five minutes, an eight-year-old for eight minutes. Keep that in mind at points in the homily when you are doing the talking, for example, during a non-participatory story. That's why these homilies incorporate lots of movement and interaction.

- *There are more people involved than you and the children.* The parishioners listen and participate along with the children. Face the parishioners as you sit down to present the homily. Speak loudly, slowly and clearly. Repeat answers given by children if the children speak too softly for the parishioners to hear. If you use a poster or another prop, make it big enough—and hold it up high enough—for the parishioners to see, too. If children participate in actions (other than in a circle or semicircle facing inward), face them toward the parishioners. While you and the children are not performing for the parishioners, you do invite them to worship with you. Keep that in mind.

- *Respect what children say.* You don't need to correct the children, you need only allow them to experience the story for themselves, to find their own meaning and, if they wish, to articulate that meaning. God reveals God's self to children, as to adults, in the right ways at the right times. Trust God to do this in your children's homilies.

In the homily, affirm all children for their responses; a simple thank-you accomplishes this beautifully. You can also say, "Jared, you believe..." or "Deanna, you feel like..," reflecting back to children what they have shared. Acknowledge each child's right to believe and feel whatever he or she believes and feels without editorializing. At times you may be hoping the children suggest a specific idea; if they do not, simply suggest the idea yourself. Your ideas matter, too, and the children want to hear them.

- *Expect the unexpected.* In these homilies you invite open responses from creative, uninhibited children. You cannot control what they say or do (nor would you want to). If they perceive you as a caring friend, they will want to tell you about their pets, toys, eating habits and other topics that you may prefer not to discuss when you are leading in front of your parishioners. This will happen. Expect it, flow with it and enjoy it. Welcome even off-the-wall comments with grace and good humor, but be cautious not to laugh at the children, even when the parishioners do. A child can easily feel hurt if a serious comment shared in trust is met with laughter. Show your respect for the children by responding appreciatively to whatever they say.

Deal with the unexpected comment by acknowledging the child and redirecting attention back to the story or activity. If a child continues, you can thank him or her for the desire to share and explain that now you would like to focus on the activity or story at hand. Ask the child, "May I listen to your story later, after church?" Be sure to follow through with the child later. You might also put your finger to you lips and say, "This is our quiet time, our time to listen to the story. Can you do that for us?"

It always helps to remember: The clearest message to the children does not come through the content of your homily, but through the loving relationship you offer them when you gather together.

On Sunday morning, make sure to bring your collected materials and this book. Take a few minutes for a final review. Place any needed materials unobtrusively near the area where you will gather the children.

We recommend that you gather at the front of the church. Children can sit in a semicircle around you on the floor. If the floor is not carpeted, consider purchasing a large square carpet remnant to make sitting more comfortable. Many churches have several low steps at the front of the church; you could sit on one of these or on a low stool. You could, of course, also sit with the children on the floor.

Once you and the children settle in, begin the homily. Look with love and respect at each young face before you. You are in for a treat: these children have invited you into a most sacred circle. Consider yourself honored ...and see what God will do.

Dirk deVries
Senior Editor

1 Samuel 1

**"If you give me a son, I promise
that I will dedicate him to you for
his whole life and that he will
never have his hair cut." (1 Samuel
1:11b, *Today's English Version*)**

Summary

In this reading from the first book of
Samuel, Hannah keeps her promise to
dedicate her son to serve God. In
today's homily, children hear today's
story and sing Hannah's song of
praise.

Materials

Bible
large poster board
felt marker
music (and music leader) for "Singing
   Hannah's Song" (printed following
   the homily on page 13; this page can
   be removed from the book)

Before the homily, copy onto poster
board the words of "Singing Hannah's
Song," printed on page 13.

Homily

Invite the children to come forward
and sit in a semicircle around you.

Hold your Bible open to the first book
of Samuel as you tell today's story:

**A long time ago, there was a man
named Elkanah who had two
wives, Hannah and Penninah.
Penninah had children but
Hannah didn't.**

**Penninah teased Hannah because
she didn't have children.**

Pause to ask:
- Have you ever been teased about
   something?
- How did that feel?
- How do you think Hannah felt
   when Penninah teased her?

Acknowledge the children's responses, then continue the story:

**Hannah wanted to have a child
very much. Sometimes she would
cry when Penninah teased her.
Elkanah tried to make her feel better, but Hannah was still sad.**

**Elkanah took his whole family to
Shiloh, to the place where people
worshiped God. While they were
there, Hannah prayed that God
would bless her with a son. She
made God a promise:**

**"God, if you will bless me with a
son, I promise that I will bring
him here to Shiloh to be a helper
for the priests. He will serve you
and he will never cut his hair."**

Again pause and ask:
- Have you ever heard a promise like
   that before?
- Why do you think Hannah made
   those promises?

■ What could it mean that someone would never cut his hair?

■ How would that person look?

Acknowledge the children's responses and continue:

A person's hair would get long if he never had it cut, wouldn't it? That's one way that people in Hannah's time could tell that someone was a servant of God for his whole life: he would have really long hair.

God heard Hannah's prayer and her promise. God blessed Hannah and Elkanah with a son. They named him Samuel.

Hannah was very happy. She sang a song about God blessing her. Hannah kept her promise. When Samuel was old enough, Hannah took him to God's house. Samuel served God through his whole life.

In today's story, Hannah prayed to ask God for a son. When her son was born, she sang a song to thank God.

There is a song that reminds me of what Hannah sang. I'd like to teach it to you. We can all sing it together. It's called "Singing Hannah's Song."

Sing the first line of the song, then repeat the line, inviting children to sing with you. Continue this "echoing" for the entire song.

You may use one, two or all three verses as your time permits. If you wish, invite the assembly to sing with you.

Prayer

God, you hear us when we pray and sing. We ask you for many things. Help us remember to thank you for all you give us. *Amen*.

Thank the children for joining you and invite them to return to their seats.

SINGING HANNAH'S SONG

O God, be praised for what you've done; At
I know the world be - longs to you. Your
Glo - ry and hon - or, thanks and praise, I

last you've blessed me with a son. I of - fer him to
care for it makes all things new. The proud are put in-
sing to you through all my days. Now fill my heart with

serve you now, And to your will a - lone we bow.
to their place; The hum - ble lift ed by your grace.
joy and peace; My wor - ship - ing will nev - er cease.

Text: J.H. Small, 1996
Music: Louis Bourgeois, 1551

1 Samuel 3:1-10

Samuel answered, "Speak; your servant is listening." (1 Samuel 3:10b, *Today's English Version*)

Summary

In this reading from the first book of Samuel, God calls to young Samuel in the middle of the night. In today's homily, children hear the story, experiment with calling someone, and discuss ways in which we respond when God calls us.

Materials

Bible
a bag
a telephone

Before the homily hide the telephone in the bag.

Homily

Invite the children to come forward and sit in a semicircle around you.

Begin the homily by discussing:
- Imagine that you wanted to talk to me, but I wasn't here.
- What would you do?

Invite children's responses. When a child suggests calling you on the telephone, take the telephone out of the bag and invite a volunteer or two to show you how they would call you on the telephone.

Ask:
- Who have you called lately?
- Who has called you lately?

- Do we always know right away whose voice we are hearing when we are on the phone?
- Not always. Sometimes we have to listen very carefully to hear who is calling.
- Today's story is about a boy— maybe just your age—who heard a voice calling and didn't know who it was. Let's listen and see if we can figure out who is calling.

Open the Bible to 1 Samuel as you tell today's story:

Once there was a young boy named Samuel. He was a helper at the Temple. The Temple was the place people went to worship, like our church.

In the Temple, Samuel worked for the high priest, Eli. Eli had been a priest for a long, long time. He had trouble seeing, so he often called Samuel to help him.

One night, Samuel snuggled down in his warm bed, fast asleep. Suddenly he woke up. What was that? He listened hard. "Samuel," called a soft voice. "Samuel."

It must be Eli, Samuel thought. But so late at night? Samuel went to see what Eli wanted.

But when Samuel got to Eli's room, he was fast asleep! Samuel

15

shook him gently, and when Eli woke up, Samuel asked, "What did you want, Eli?"

"What? Want?" Eli rubbed his eyes. "Nothing, Samuel. Why?"

"Didn't you call me?" Samuel asked.

"No, Samuel. Now go back to bed!" Eli rolled over and immediately started snoring.

Samuel walked back to his room and climbed back into bed.

Then he heard it again, "Samuel. Samuel." He scrambled out of bed again and trotted to Eli's room. "Yes, Eli?"

"What, Samuel? Is it you again? I didn't call you."

Samuel went back to his room, but this time he sat on his bed and waited, and, sure enough, the voice called to him once again: "Samuel, Samuel!" It *must* be Eli! Who else would call him?

He again returned to Eli, who this time was waiting for him. "No, Samuel, I am not calling you, but I think I know who is. I think *God*

is calling you. Next time, when you hear the voice, answer, 'Speak, Lord, your servant is listening.'"

And that's exactly what Samuel did.

SPEAK, LORD, FOR YOUR SERVANT HEARS.
I SAMUEL

Discuss with the children:
- Why do you think God called Samuel?
- How did Samuel respond when he finally realized it was God who was calling?
- How do you think God calls us today?
- What do you think God wants to say to us?
- If God called our names today, how would we respond?

Prayer

Thank you, God, for calling each of us by name. Help us to listen when you call. *Amen*.

Thank the children for joining you and invite them to return to their seats.

16

1 Samuel 16:1-13

Samuel took the olive oil and anointed David in front of his brothers. (1 Samuel 16:13a, *Today's English Version*)

Summary

In this reading from the first book of Samuel, Samuel follows God's instruction to anoint the next king of Israel. In today's homily, children will touch, smell and taste olives and olive oil, hear today's story and talk about how David was anointed to be king.

Materials

Bible
grocery bag containing:
- small can of black olives, drained as close to the time of your homily as possible
- small cruet or other container of olive oil
- paper towels or napkins

Homily

Invite the children to come forward and sit in a semicircle around you.

Show the children the can of drained olives and ask:
- Do you know what this is?
- Have you eaten this food before?

Give each child an olive. Invite the children to examine the olives, their smell, feel and taste. Discuss:
- How does the olive smell? taste?
- Does olive oil come out of the olive?

Show the children the container of olive oil. Let them smell the oil, dip a fingertip into it and taste it, if they wish. Discuss:
- It takes a lot of olives to make olive oil.
- In Bible times, olive oil was used for cooking, as fuel for lamps, as a medicine, as a sacrifice and for anointing. Anointing someone meant smearing some oil on that person's forehead. Sometimes the oil was poured over the person's head.
- What would feel like to have this oil poured on your head? How would you look? Would your face look shiny?

That happened to David when Samuel anointed him to be king of Israel.

Hold your Bible open to the first book of Samuel as you tell today's story:

Saul was king of Israel, but he wasn't doing what God wanted. God told Samuel, the prophet, to go to Bethlehem and find a man named Jesse who had eight sons. God told Samuel that one of Jesse's sons would be the one chosen to be the next king.

When Samuel met Jesse, he didn't know which of Jesse's sons he should anoint.

17

"This one is handsome," thought Samuel.

God said, "No, he's not the one."

"This one is tall and strong," thought Samuel.

God said, "No, he's not the one."

Seven of Jesse's sons came to Samuel, and every time God said, "No, he's not the one."

Samuel was tired. "Do you have any more sons?" he asked.

Jesse told Samuel that his youngest son, David, was out taking care of the sheep.

Samuel said, "Well, send for him; I'd better see them all."

Jesse called for David, and when he arrived, God told Samuel, "That's the one! Anoint him!"

Samuel poured olive oil on David's head. God's spirit filled him.

After Saul died, David became a great king for God's people.

Prayer

Great God, you chose David to be a king. We thank you for choosing us to be your people. Help us to follow you and fill us with your Spirit. *Amen.*

Collect any olives, toweling, etc., from the children and put them away for disposal later.

Thank the children for joining you and invite them to return to their seats.

1 Samuel 17:1-54

David strapped Saul's sword over the armor and tried to walk, but he couldn't because he wasn't used to wearing them. "I can't fight with all this," he said to Saul. "I'm not used to it." So he took it all off. (1 Samuel 16:39b, *Today's English Version*)

Summary

In this reading from the first book of Samuel, David becomes a hero by defeating the Philistines' champion, Goliath. In today's homily, children wear things that are "too big," hear today's story and discover that God's care fits us "just right."

Materials

items of clothing that will be too large for the children, for example, a man's shirt, women's shoes (but not high heels!), a large hat, a large ring, etc.

Homily

Invite the children to come forward and sit in a semicircle around you.

Begin the homily by asking:
■ Have you ever played "dress up"?
■ What do you pretend when you dress up? What characters do you like to be?

Show the children the items you brought and invite volunteers to dress up in them. If you have more volun-teers than items to try, and you have time, pass around the dress-up items.

Ask the children wearing the dress-up items:
■ How do those things feel?
■ How do you feel wearing them?

Ask the other children:
■ Describe how the children wearing the items look.

Ask all the children:
■ What might happen next if you played a game of dress up with these clothes?
■ If you dressed up in these clothes, would you be able to play on a swing? to do chores at home? to go to school? Why or why not?
■ Today's story is about a boy named David. Someone wanted him to wear the wrong clothes! Let's listen and see what kind of clothes they were.

Hold your Bible open to the first book of Samuel as you tell today's story:

David was the youngest of eight brothers. David was home tending sheep while some his brothers

were with King Saul in Israel's army. The army was fighting the Philistines. Instead of having lots of people fighting, the Philistines challenged Israel to send one man to fight their champion, Goliath.

Day after day, morning and night, Goliath called out his dare: "Here I am! Can't you find *one* man who isn't afraid to fight me?" Goliath was so big that no one in Saul's army wanted to volunteer, not even Saul himself!

David's father, Jesse, sent him to take food to his brothers. When David saw his brothers, they teased him, "What are you doing here? Did you come to play soldier? Who is watching your sheep?"

Later, David saw Goliath and heard him challenge the army. Still no one volunteered.

Even though David was young and small, and he wasn't in the army, he said he would fight Goliath. At first, the soldiers laughed at him, but David explained, "When I take care of my sheep, I have to fight big animals to keep the sheep safe. God takes care of me then, and God will take care of me if I fight Goliath."

Since no one else wanted to fight Goliath, Saul finally agreed to let David try. King Saul gave David his armor and his weapons, but they were too big and heavy for David. He struggled to put them on! David couldn't fight in Saul's clothes.

David believed that God would take care of him just the way he was. God's love was like a shield that fit David just right. God protected David and helped him face Goliath. David won the fight.

King Saul, the soldiers and all Israel celebrated. They knew that David's faith in God was right. David became a great hero that day by believing in God and by believing in himself.

Ask:
- What do you think would have happened if David had worn Saul's armor to fight Goliath?
- Why did David believe God would take care of him?
- Do you ever face things that look too big to handle, problems too big to figure out?
- Does God's love come in different sizes?
- I think God's love is always the right size for us!

Prayer

Holy God, we know you will take care of us even when our problems look bigger than we are. Help us to trust you always. *Amen.*

Thank the children for joining you and invite them to return to their seats.

1 Samuel 20:1-42

**"May the Lord be with you as he was
with my father!"** (1 Samuel 20:13b,
Today's English Version)

Summary

In this reading from the first book of
Samuel, Jonathan helps David escape
King Saul's anger. In today's homily,
children identify symbols that warn of
danger, hear today's story and discuss
what it means to be a friend.

Materials

Bible
several objects with warning symbols
on them, for example, a skull and
crossbones, a no-swimming sign, a
stop sign, etc.
bow and arrow (if you don't have
these, a picture of a bow and arrow
will also work)

Homily

Invite the children to come forward
and have them sit in a semicircle
around you.

Show the children the warning symbols, one at a time. Ask what each
means, acknowledging guesses and
repeating correct suggestions. After
the symbols have all been identified,
ask:
■ What do all of these symbols have
in common?

Show the bow and arrow. Ask:
■ What are these?
■ Do they have something in common with the warning signals we
saw?

I'm going to tell you a story about
how a bow and arrow became a way
of warning a friend about danger.

Hold your Bible open to the first book
of Samuel as you tell today's story:

**David and Jonathan were best
friends. Each of them was very
good at using a weapon. David
was good at using a slingshot and
Jonathan was good at using a bow
and arrow.**

**Jonathan's father, Saul, was king
of Israel. That meant that Jonathan was the "crown prince"; he
would be king after his father
died.**

**But God decided that David should
be king after Saul, instead of
Jonathan. Now that *might* have
made Jonathan angry or jealous,
but it didn't. Jonathan wanted
David to be his friend more than
he wanted to be king.**

***Saul* was angry and jealous,
though. He was afraid David might
take the throne away from him.
He was so afraid that he wanted to
get rid of David, even if that meant
killing him.**

**David knew he was in danger. He
asked Jonathan to help him:
"Jonathan, I don't want to have
dinner with King Saul tonight. If**

21

he asks where I am, please tell him I've gone to my father's house. If that makes him angry, you'll know he wanted to hurt me."

"David, you are my best friend. I promise that I will tell you if my father wants to hurt you. Hide in the field behind the big pile of rocks tomorrow. If my father says anything about hurting you, I will warn you.

"Here's what I'll do: I'll bring my bow and arrow to the field. If it is safe for you to come to my house, I'll shoot the arrow so it lands in front of the rocks. If it is not safe, I'll shoot the arrow past the rocks."

That night, at dinner, Jonathan learned that his father wanted to get rid of David. Saul wanted *Jonathan* to be the next king, not David. Saul even got angry at Jonathan when he tried to explain that it was more important for him to be David's friend than to be king.

The next day, Jonathan took his bow and arrow to the field. He shot the arrow past the rocks, just as he promised. When David came out of his hiding place, he and Jonathan were both very sad. They knew David had to leave to be safe. And he did. He went away and didn't come back for a long time.

Jonathan kept his promise to David. He warned his friend and made sure that David would live to become king someday.

Ask:
- How do you think David felt when he saw the arrow go past the rock?
- How do you think Jonathan felt?
- Being a good friend isn't always easy, is it? Sometimes it's hard to be a friend.
- How can we help our friends?
- Remember that our friends can be people our own age, or our teachers, our pastors, our parents, our brothers and sisters, our grandparents. *(If you feel comfortable doing so, remind the children that you are their friend, too.)*
- Being a good friend is like a gift, one you give to another person and also one you give to yourself.
- Let's thank God for our friends.

Prayer

Holy God, we thank you for our friends. Help us to take care of each other. We pray in your name. *Amen.*

Thank the children for sharing with you and invite them to return to their seats.

■ ■ ■ ■ ■

1 Samuel 24:1-22;
26:1-25

"The Lord rewards those who are faithful and righteous." (1 Samuel 26:23a, *Today's English Version*)

Summary

In this reading from the first book of Samuel, David spares Saul's life. In today's homily, children act out the story, then discuss what it means to be a leader.

Materials

Bible
a fancy sign that reads *Leader*
small cups, equal to half the number of children
masking tape, yarn or rope

Homily

Invite the children to come forward and sit around you in a semicircle.

Begin the homily by discussing:
■ Imagine that you wanted to be leader of our group.
■ The leader of our group gets to hold this sign. *(Show children the Leader sign,)*
■ What could you do to get this sign?
■ Today we are going to act out a story about David and Saul.
■ Saul was king of Israel but he wasn't doing what God wanted.
■ David had been chosen to take over as leader of Israel but Saul didn't like that idea.
■ Let's see what happened:

Divide the children into two groups, *Davids* and *Sauls*. Give each *Saul* a water jar (paper cup). Explain:
■ When Saul is ready to go to sleep, he will place the water jar next to his head.
■ Saul will not wake up until he hears David say, "Where is the king's water jar?"

Place the tape, yarn or rope on the floor to show the valley between David and Saul.

Place the *Leader* sign on the Saul side of the valley. (Or have a child hold the sign, if necessary.)

Continue:
■ *Sauls*, go to that side of the valley. *(Indicate the Saul side.)*
■ *Davids*, stand on this side of the valley. *(Indicate the David side.)*
■ All of you, listen carefully so you can act out your part of the story!

Hold your Bible open to the first book of Samuel as you tell today's story:

Once there was a man named Saul. He was a very proud man. *(Look proud, Sauls.)*

Saul was king of all Israel, but he wasn't very happy. *(Look sad, Sauls.)*

23

Saul was afraid that someone was going to take his place as leader. That someone was David. *(Look strong,* Davids.)

Saul and David both knew that God wanted David to be leader. *(Everybody nod.)* But Saul didn't like that idea. *(Everybody shake heads side to side.)*

Saul tried looking for David, to run him out of Israel and get rid of him for good. *(Look with your hand above your eyes,* Sauls.)

David was hiding in the mountains, on one side of a valley. *(Duck down,* Davids.)

When Saul found where David was hiding, he set up his camp on the opposite side of a valley, and went to sleep for the night. (Sauls, *put your water jars at your heads and go to sleep.)*

While Saul was sleeping, David crossed the valley. *(Tiptoe to the other side,* Davids.)

David could have become leader then—he could have taken the sign from Saul. *(Look closely at the sign,* Davids.) But David didn't do that. (Davids, *shake your heads side to side.)* Instead, David took the water jar that was beside Saul's head. *(Take the jars,* Davids.) Then David went back to his camp. *(Cross the valley again,* Davids.)

When David was safely back in his camp, he shouted, "Where is the king's water jar?" *(Shout,* Davids.)

Saul and everyone in his camp woke up. They were very surprised! *(Look surprised,* Sauls.)

Saul saw that his water jar was gone! Saul knew that David had been right next to him. Saul knew that David could have become leader but he didn't.

Saul was glad that David didn't hurt him. *(Wipe your forehead,* Sauls.) But he was also ashamed that he'd tried to hurt David. *(Look sorry,* Sauls.)

He called to David and said, "David, I have been wrong to fight with you. I will never fight with you again."

David called back, "The Lord rewards those who are faithful and righteous."

David meant that he didn't have to take anything from Saul. He would wait for God to make him leader when the time was right. That made David feel good. *(Smile,* Davids.)

Saul called out, "May God bless you!" *(Smile,* Sauls.)

Then David and Saul each went home.

Prayer

Thank you, God, for leaders. Help our leaders to be wise and patient. We pray in your name. *Amen.*

Thank the children for helping you tell the story. Ask for their help collecting cups, sign and tape, and invite them to return to their seats.

■ ■ ■ ■ ■

2 Samuel
11:26–12:10, 13-15

"You are that man," Nathan said to David. (2 Samuel 12:7a, *Today's English Version*)

Summary

In this reading from the second book of Samuel, Nathan the prophet tells a parable to King David. In today's homily, children first look into a mirror and discuss the ways we see ourselves and others; they then hear today's story.

Materials

a mirror in a bag
a Bible

Homily

Invite the children to come forward and sit around you in a semicircle.

Begin the homily by discussing:
■ If you were going somewhere and you wanted to make sure your hair was combed and your face was clean, what would you do?

When a child mentions using a mirror, take the mirror from the bag. Pass the mirror around. Ask:
■ Are there other ways you would be able to find out how you looked?

When a child mentions asking another person to tell you how you look, say:
■ Sometimes *a person* can act like a mirror. A person can tell you something about yourself that you need to know.

■ That happened in today's Bible story. Let's listen.

Hold your Bible open to the second book of Samuel as you tell today's story:

David was King of Israel. In David's time, men sometimes had more than one wife. David had many wives. He was very rich and he lived in a palace in Jerusalem with all his wives and children.

On the other side of Jerusalem, there lived a man named Uriah. Uriah was a soldier in David's army. Uriah's wife was Bathsheba. She was very beautiful.

One day, David saw Bathsheba sunbathing and fell in love with her. He wanted to marry her but she was already married to Uriah. David thought about this, and he came up with a plan.

David knew that if Uriah died in a battle, then Bathsheba could marry him. So David sent Uriah to the place where the army was fighting. Uriah was killed in the battle.

David married Bathsheba.

The Bible tells stories about real people; some of the things they do

aren't nice at all. This is a sad story, isn't it? Let's hear what else happened.

After David and Bathsheba married, a prophet named Nathan came to visit the king. A prophet was a person who brought a message from God. A prophet's message usually reminded God's people to care for each other and to follow God's laws.

Why do you think Nathan came to visit David?

Nathan told David a story. It was a special kind of story called a parable. The parable was this:

A poor man had one lamb. He loved the lamb and took very good care of it. A rich man had lots of lambs, but when he wanted to have a feast, instead of using one of his own lambs to feed his guests, the rich man stole the poor man's one lamb. The poor man's lamb became the rich man's dinner.

How do you think the poor man felt? What do you think of the rich man? What do you think should happen to him?

When David heard this story, he was angry.

"That's a terrible thing!" David shouted. "That rich man deserves to be punished! He has to pay back four times what he took!"

Nathan looked at David very carefully and said, *"You* are the man."

David was shocked. "What do you mean?"

Nathan told David the whole story about Uriah and Bathsheba. "God blessed you, David. And God would have given you more if what you had wasn't enough. Instead, you stole the one lamb, Bathsheba, from Uriah."

How do you think David felt when he heard this? How was Nathan like a mirror for David?

(Hold up the mirror and say:) Nathan helped David see that he'd done something wrong. David was sorry for what he'd done. God forgave David. David's life wasn't always happy, but he knew that God loved him.

Discuss:
- Has someone ever helped you to see something you shouldn't have done? How did that feel?
- We don't always like being shown when we've been wrong, but when someone acts like a mirror for us, it can help us.
- God loves us, even when we make mistakes. Even if the mistakes are big ones, God forgives us.
- We should remember to forgive others, too.

Prayer

God, we know that you love us. Help us to look at ourselves and ask for forgiveness when we are wrong. *Amen*.

Thank the children for joining in today's homily and invite them to return to their seats.

■ ■ ■ ■ ■

1 Kings 3:5-12

**"So give me the wisdom I need to
rule your people with justice and
to know the difference between
good and evil." (1 Kings 3:9a,
Today's English Version)**

Summary

In this reading from the first book of
Kings, God invites Solomon to ask for
a gift. In today's homily, children
choose gifts, discuss making choices
and hear today's story.

Materials

Bible
option 1:
small, inexpensive items (for example,
    pencils or stickers) to give the chil-
    dren, each in its own box, each
    wrapped as a gift (Note: The gifts
    themselves should be identical, but
    wrap them in boxes of differing
    sizes with varying papers.)
option 2:
3 or 4 packages of different sizes,
    wrapped in different papers

Homily

Invite the children to come forward
and sit in a semicircle around you.

Ask:
■ How many of us like to get gifts?
■ How would someone know what
    sort of gift to give you for your
    birthday or for Christmas?
■ Can you think of a gift that was
    really special to you? What was it?
    Why was it special?

■ I brought several gifts along today.
    If I gave you a chance to choose
    one, which would you choose?
    Why?

If using *option 1*, ask each child to
choose a gift. After children select
their gifts, explain that the gifts in the
boxes are all the same. Ask children to
place their *unopened* gifts on the
floor in front of them until the end of
the homily.

If using *option 2,* ask children briefly
to discuss which of the three or four
packages they would most like to
receive as a gift.

Say:
■ Today's story is about choosing a
    gift.

Hold your Bible open to the first book
of Kings as you tell today's story:

**Once there was a man named
Solomon who became king of
Israel. Solomon's father, David,
had been a great king. Solomon
wanted to be like his father.**

**One night, God came to Solomon
in a dream.**

**God said, "Solomon, what gift
would you like me to give you?"**

27

Imagine that! Solomon was invited to ask God for anything!

What would *we* have asked for?

Let's hear what Solomon really did ask for:

Solomon thought about all the things he could ask from God.

"I could ask for money...but I'm already rich; I could ask for power ...but I'm already the king; I could ask for love...but I already have wives and children."

Solomon thought some more. And then he knew!

"God, I am the ruler of your people. I'm young and have lots to learn. Give me wisdom so I can rule your people fairly. Help me to know the difference between right and wrong so I can be a good king."

God gave Solomon wisdom. God was very pleased that Solomon asked for something that would be good for his people, not just for himself.

God also blessed Solomon with the things he didn't ask for: wealth and honor, and a long life.

When Solomon woke up, he realized God had spoken to him in the dream. He went to the place where his people worshiped and thanked God for blessing him.

Ask:
- What do you think of Solomon's dream?
- Did Solomon choose the best gift?
- What made Solomon's choice a good one?

Prayer

God, you are the one who gives all gifts. Thank you for all you give us. Help us to make good choices and to think about giving to others. *Amen.*

If using *option 1,* invite the children to take their gifts with them to open after the service.

Thank the children for joining you and invite them to return to their seats.

28

■ ■ ■ ■ ■

1 Kings 3:16-28

**They were all filled with deep respect
for him... (1 Kings 3:28b, *Today's
English Version*)**

Summary

In this reading from the first book of
Kings, Solomon faces a difficult decision. In today's homily, children hear
the story and discuss decisions.

Materials

Bible
balloon in a paper bag

Homily

Invite the children to come forward
and sit in a semicircle around you.

Begin the homily by discussing:
- If two people want the same thing,
  like an apple or a piece of cake,
  what could they do?

When a child suggests cutting the item
in half, take the balloon from the bag.
Ask:
- What about this? Could we cut this
  in half? Why not?
- What are some *other* things that
  can't be cut in half and shared?
- What might happen if two people
  wanted the same thing, something
  like the balloon, that couldn't be
  divided?
- Today's story is about two people
  who wanted the same thing.

Open your Bible to the first book of
Kings. Hold the balloon as you tell the
story:

Israel's King Solomon was a very
wise man. People came from
all over to ask him questions.
Sometimes people came to
Solomon for help in settling their
arguments.

One day, two women came to
Solomon with a very big problem.

The first woman spoke:

> King Solomon, this woman and
> I live in the same house. Each
> of us had a baby boy. My baby
> was born two days before hers,
> so they were the same size and
> they looked a lot alike.
>
> The other night, her baby died.
> She took my baby and put her
> child in his place. At first, even
> I thought my baby was the one
> who died. But I looked very
> closely and now I know what
> happened.
>
> I feel sorry for this woman, but
> I want my baby back!

*(Pause in the homily and move to
the other side of the semicircle to
show that you are speaking for
the other woman.)*

The second woman told Solomon
the story she wanted him to hear:

That's not true, your Majesty. This baby is mine! I'm not going to give him back to her. Please let me keep the baby.

The women argued back and forth for a while. Solomon thought and thought.

What do you think Solomon said? How did he decide who was the baby's mother?

Solomon called for his sword. He said, "If you both say this healthy baby is yours, I will divide him so you can each have half."

The baby's real mother loved her child so much that she didn't want him cut in half!

"Oh no! King Solomon," she cried, "give the baby to the other woman, but please don't hurt him!"

Solomon knew the woman was the baby's real mother, and he gave her the baby.

When the people in Israel heard how Solomon decided the argument between these women, they knew that God had blessed him with great wisdom.

Ask:
■ What do you think of Solomon's idea to cut the baby in half?
■ How did that idea help him find out who was the real mother?
■ God blessed Solomon with wisdom. That was good for Solomon. How was it also good for the people of Israel?
■ Who makes hard decisions today?
■ Who do you think needs wisdom, like Solomon?
■ When might *we* need wisdom, like Solomon?

Prayer

Holy God, you are the one who helps us make good decisions. Guide our leaders and make them wise. *Amen.*

Thank the children for joining you and invite them to return to their seats.

■ ■ ■ ■ ■

1 Kings 6–8

"Not even all of heaven is large enough to hold you, so how can this Temple that I have built be large enough?" (1 Kings 8:27b, *Today's English Version*)

Summary

In this reading from the first book of Kings, Solomon builds a Temple to be God's house in Jerusalem. In today's homily, children tour their worship space, talk about the places where God is found and hear today's story.

Materials

Bible
pictures of churches, synagogues, other houses of worship
drawing of what Solomon's temple may have looked like (found at the end of the homily on page 33; cut this page out to use in the homily)

Before the homily:
■ Plan a simple, quick "tour" of your worship space.
■ Practice the tour to make sure the timing is appropriate.
■ Gather interesting information about your church building, for example:
　— When was it constructed?
　— What materials were used?
　— If there are donated items, who gave them and when?
■ Ask your pastor (or your church historian, if you have one) for these stories. You might enlist the pastor or historian to help as a guest com-

mentator for the "tour" portion of the homily.

Homily

Invite the children to come forward and sit in a semicircle around you.

Begin the homily by discussing:
■ Tell me about your houses. What do they look like?
■ What are our favorite rooms in our houses? Why?
■ Where do you think God lives?

Show the pictures of worship places and continue:
■ Here are some places where God lives. Every house of God is special. No two are alike.
■ Does God live here in our church? Let's take a tour of this house of God!

Conduct the "tour."

After the tour, have the children sit in a semicircle. Hold your Bible open to the first book of Kings as you tell today's story:

When Solomon was king of Israel, he had many great buildings built. One of the most important buildings was a house for God.

God's house in Jerusalem was called the Temple. It was made from huge cedar and pine trees from Lebanon. The Temple had paneled walls and was decorated with beautiful carvings. There were bronze fixtures and the whole inside was covered with gold. It was very impressive!

Inside the Temple was the Covenant Box. The Covenant Box held God's laws. The Covenant Box looked a little like a throne.

Solomon built the Temple to be God's house in Jerusalem, but Solomon knew that God didn't live in just one place. Solomon's Temple was a place where God's people gathered to worship.

Solomon led a celebration to dedicate the Temple to God. The people were glad because they could see the place where God lived among them.

God lives among us too.

Ask:
- Is any place big enough to hold God?
- Is any place too small for God?
- God is in our hearts—very small places—and God is in worship places—as big as ours and bigger!

Prayer

God, we thank you for being in this place. Help us remember that no place is too small or too big for you. *Amen.*

Thank the children for joining you for today's homily and invite them to return to their seats.

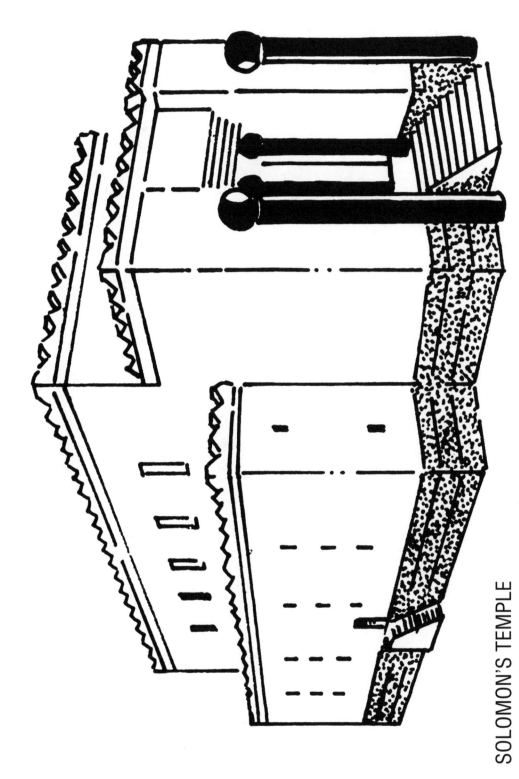

SOLOMON'S TEMPLE

1 Kings 17:8-16

As the Lord had promised through Elijah, the bowl did not run out of flour nor did the jar run out of oil.
(1 Kings 17:16, *Today's English Version*)

Summary

In this reading from the first book of Kings, a miracle saves Elijah, a widow and her son. In today's homily, children hear this story, taste bread and discuss sharing.

Materials

Bible
pita or other flatbread, enough for
  each child to sample
large sheet of newsprint or poster
  board
felt marker

Homily

Invite the children to come forward and sit in a semicircle around you.

Begin the homily by discussing:
■ Imagine that you were going to make bread. What would you need?

Use the paper and marker to list the items that children suggest. Review the list. Make sure it includes *flour, water, salt* and *oil*. Continue:
■ Some bread has yeast to make it rise. Some bread is flat.
■ Some bread is soft; some is crunchy.
■ I've brought some bread to share with you today. This is pita bread (or flatbread).

Distribute the bread. Invite the children to look at it, feel it and taste it. Ask the children to save a bit of the bread to share with someone at the end of the homily.

Ask:
■ Have you eaten this type of bread before?
■ How is it different from other bread you've eaten?
■ This bread is made from flour, water, oil and salt. There is no yeast in it to make it fluffy.
■ Bread was, and is, a very important food. People all over the world eat some type of bread. That's true now and it was true for the people whose stories we read about in the Bible. There are lots of stories in the Bible that have to do with people making and eating bread.
■ Today's Bible story is about a man named Elijah and the bread he ate. Elijah's bread was a lot like what you're eating now. Think about that while I tell you his story.

Hold your Bible open to the first book of Kings as you tell today's story:

Elijah was a prophet. A prophet was someone who heard a message from God and then told other people about it.

There was no rain in Israel. Without rain, plants wouldn't grow and people wouldn't have much food.

God sent Elijah to stay with a widow and her son. God promised Elijah that the woman would give him food while he stayed there. Elijah went to her town, a long way off. When he got there, he found her gathering wood.

"Widow," Elijah called, "I've traveled a long way. Please bring me a drink of water."

The woman started to get Elijah some water. He called to her again.

"And please bring me some bread, too. I'm hungry!

The widow turned at stared at Elijah. She was tired and sad. She was even a little angry.

"What! You want me to bring you bread? I don't *have* any bread. I came here to get firewood to bake a last loaf of bread for me and my son. My bowl has one handful of flour and my jar just a little olive oil. Once we've eaten that, we'll starve."

The woman's story made Elijah feel sorry for her. Elijah believed God's promise that the widow would be able to give him food.

"Don't worry," Elijah said. "God has promised to provide enough for all of us. Go home and make the bread. Make a small loaf for me and the rest for you and your son. You'll have enough flour and enough oil to feed us all until the drought ends."

The widow went to her house and did what Elijah told her to do. She was amazed. There was enough flour and oil to make the bread that day...and the next day...and the next day...

Discuss with the children:
■ Have you ever been asked to share something?
■ Is sharing always an easy thing to do? When is it hard to share?
■ Elijah, the widow and her son shared what God provided for them. God blessed them with a miracle.
■ If God asked you to share, what would you do? I'm going to ask you to share. Please offer some of your bread to someone else when you return to your seats.
■ But let's pray first.

Prayer

Holy God, we thank you for all you give us. Help us to share what we have. *Amen*.

Thank the children for joining you and invite them to return to their seats. Remind them to share their remaining bread with someone seated near them.

■ ■ ■ ■ ■

1 Kings 17:18-24

"Now I know that you are a man of God and that the Lord really speaks though you!" (1 Kings 17:24, *Today's English Version*)

Summary

In this reading from the first book of Kings, Elijah brings a boy back to life. In today's homily, children roleplay the story of the raising of the widow's son.

Materials

Bible
medicine bottle
bag
three scarves:
■ a hat for Elijah—use a piece of yarn or string to tie around the forehead
■ a scarf for the widow of Zarephath—tie the scarf at the chin
■ a cloak for the boy—drape around shoulders or over the torso

Before the homily, place the medicine bottle and the scarves in the bag. You may wish to enlist an adult or older child to help with the scarves.

Homily

Invite the children to come forward and sit in a semicircle around you.

Begin the homily by asking:
■ Who of us has been sick lately?
■ What helped us get better?

When a child mentions "medicine," remove the bottle from the bag. Ask:
■ What kinds of medicines are there?

■ What does medicine do?
■ Do all medicines come in a bottle? What medicine doesn't come in a bottle? *(love, laughter)*
■ Today we are going to roleplay a story from the Bible about three people: a little boy who was very sick, the little boy's mother and a prophet named Elijah.

Ask for volunteers for the three primary roles. The rest of the children will be a chorus. Explain what you would like the children to do for the roleplay:
■ Elijah, the woman and her son will act out their parts as I tell the story.
■ When I say "prophet," *Elijah* will lift his (her) eyes and hands up, looking to God for help.
■ When I say "mother," *mother* will put her (his) hands on her (his) heart.
■ When I say "boy," the *boy* will make a "thumbs up" sign.
■ The rest of us are the chorus. It's our job to listen to the story and whenever I say, "Just remember..," we say, "God's love makes all things possible!"

Practice the chorus a few times while Elijah, the widow and the boy arrange their scarves. Start with the boy's scarf draped around the shoulders like a cloak. Later it will be a cover for him as he lies in his bed.

Hold your Bible open to the first book of Kings as you begin the roleplay:

This is a story about a *boy*, his *mother* and a *prophet* named Elijah.

Elijah was living with a woman and her son in a place called Zarephath. There was no rain in the land, and the people didn't have much to eat.

When the woman or her son were worried, Elijah would say, "Just remember..."

(Chorus: "God's love makes all things possible!")

The *boy* got sick. At first his stomach hurt. Then his head hurt. Then all he wanted to do was sleep. He went to his bed and stayed there. He wasn't well at all. One day, he died.

The *mother* was very sad. She went to Elijah, crying and said, "O man of God, why did this happen?"

Elijah tried to comfort the woman. He said, "Just remember..."

(Chorus: "God's love makes all things possible!")

Elijah felt sad too. He liked the widow and her son. The *prophet* prayed to God: "O God, this woman has been kind to me. Please be kind to her in return."

Elijah touched the *boy* three times. Each time, he prayed, "God, please let this child live!"

God heard the *prophet's* prayer. Elijah was right; the woman had been kind and God blessed her.

While Elijah prayed, suddenly, the *boy* began to breathe again.

He was alive! Elijah was very happy. He called for the woman.

When the *mother* saw that the *boy* was alive and well, she thanked Elijah and she thanked God.

"I know you are a true *prophet* and from now on, whenever I'm afraid or worried, I'll think of what you said, "Just remember..."

(Chorus: "God's love makes all things possible!")

Thank the children for their participation in the roleplay. Ask those wearing the scarves to return them to you.

Discuss:
- What kind of medicine did Elijah use? *(prayer, faith, love)*
- Can we find those in bottles somewhere? Where are those things?

Prayer

Holy God, you bless us with so many gifts. Some are outside us, and some are inside us. We thank you for all of them, and ask that you help us just remember that "God makes all things possible!" *Amen*.

Thank the children for joining you and invite them to return to their seats.

1 Kings 19:1-18

When Elijah heard it, he covered his face with his cloak and went out and stood at the entrance of the cave. A voice said to him, "Elijah, what are you doing here?" (1 Kings 19:13, *Today's English Version*)

Summary

In this reading from the first book of Kings, Elijah runs away to Mount Sinai where he meets God in a new way. In today's homily, children discuss meeting someone and provide "special effects" for the telling of the story.

Materials

Bible

Homily

Invite the children to come forward and sit in a semicircle around you.

Begin the homily by discussing:
- Imagine we were all strangers. We've never met before. How would you introduce yourself to another person?
- What if you couldn't use your name? How would you introduce yourself?
- What if you couldn't use words at all? How would you tell us something about who you are?

In response to this final question, invite volunteers to demonstrate their wordless introductions.

Hold your Bible open to the first book of Kings as you tell today's story:

Once there was a man named Elijah. He was a prophet, a man who listened to God's voice and shared God's words with other people.

But sometimes people didn't want to hear what Elijah had to say.

That's what happened when Elijah went to the king and queen of Israel. They had been worshiping idols. Idols are things that people put ahead of God, want more than God, love more than God.

"Stop worshiping those idols!" Elijah demanded. "Worship the real God. If you don't, you are sinning."

Elijah's message made the king and queen angry. The queen was so angry, she wanted to have Elijah killed!

Jezebel the queen sent out a command: "Find that prophet, Elijah, and kill him. It's either him or me!"

Elijah was scared. He ran away into the desert. It was dry and hot. Elijah though he might die in the desert, but at least Queen Jezebel wouldn't follow him there.

Elijah found a small tree and laid down in the shade to cool off and rest. While he was sleeping, God sent an angel with food and water for Elijah. "Wake up, Elijah! Here's some food for you." Elijah woke, saw the bread and the water jar and ate the meal. Then he went back to sleep.

God sent the angel again with more food and water. "Wake up, Elijah! You have to eat and drink enough to keep you strong for a long time."

Elijah woke up again, saw the food and ate and drank. The food made him very strong, strong enough to walk all the way to a mountain called Sinai—and that was a long, long walk!

Elijah found a cave in the mountain and went inside to sleep. Suddenly, he heard a voice. It was God! "Elijah, what are you doing here?"

Elijah was very surprised. "I'm the last person who believes in you, God!"

"Go, stand on the top of the mountain," said God.

Elijah obeyed.

When he got to the top of the mountain, God sent a furious wind. *(Invite the children to make blowing noises and to sway from side to side.)*

Then God send an earthquake. *(Encourage the children to stamp their feet, making a roaring noise, and to shake.)*

Next, God sent a fire. *(Encourage children to raise their hands, wiggle their fingers and say "crackle, crackle.")*

After the fire, there was a still, small voice.

Let's whisper...whisper...whisper. *(Say the word, "whisper" in a very low voice; invite the children to join you. Make the whispering quieter and quieter.)*

"Elijah," God said, "what are you doing here?" Elijah told God the whole story about the queen wanting to kill him.

"Go back home, Elijah. I will protect you. Anoint a new king and a new prophet. They will help you carry out my work."

And that's just what Elijah did!

Elijah knew God before he went to Sinai but God was able to remind Elijah that he still had a lot to learn. Meeting God in a new way helped make Elijah brave and strong.

Prayer

God, you can meet us in so many ways. Help us to see and hear you in our daily life. We ask for you to make us brave and strong. *Amen.*

Thank the children for joining you and invite them to return to their seats.

■ ■ ■ ■ ■

1 Kings 19:19-21

Elijah took off his cloak and put it on Elisha. (1 Kings 19:19c,
Today's English Version)

Summary

In this reading from the first book of Kings, Elijah chooses Elisha to be his disciple. In today's homily, children play a brief game of Follow the Leader, hear the story and discuss what it means to be a follower.

Materials

Bible
scarf or rectangular length of cloth

Homily

Invite the children to come forward and *stand* around you in a semicircle.

Begin the homily by asking:
■ Today, we're going to play a brief game of Follow the Leader. The *leader* will be the person who is wearing this scarf around his or her shoulders.
■ There is a special part to this game: The *leader* must decide to pass along the scarf at some time. The *leader* can give the scarf to anyone he or she chooses, but a person can only be *leader* once.

The scarf does not have to be passed to another child; you, the pastor or anyone in a nearby seat is "fair game."

Begin the game. Monitor the passing of the scarf. If the *leader* remains the same for more than a minute, say:

■ It's time to pass the scarf!

Allow the game to be played for several minutes. Determine the time based on how many children are participating, as well as how long you have for the homily. For a small group, try to have each child be *leader*.

Announce the end of the game and invite the children to sit in a semicircle around you.

Discuss:
■ How did it feel to be *leader*?
■ How did you feel when you passed the scarf? when the scarf was passed to you?

Hold your Bible open to the first book of Kings as you tell today's story:

Today's story is about two men: Elijah and Elisha. Their names sound alike, don't they?

Elijah means "My God is God"; Elisha means "God is Salvation."

Elijah was a prophet. He took God's messages to people. It was a hard job because the people didn't always like what Elijah told them.

God decided to give Elijah a helper and sent him to find Elisha. When Elijah found his helper, Elisha was in a field behind a team of twelve yokes of oxen.

Who can tell us what *oxen* are? (*large work animals, like bulls*)

Who can tell us what *yokes* are? (*wooden braces holding two work animals together*)

Elijah took off his cloak and put it around Elisha. That was a way of showing that Elisha would be the next prophet, the next leader to bring God's word to the people. It meant that Elisha was Elijah's heir; sometimes a man who followed a prophet was even called that prophet's son! Elisha knew this was a great honor.

"Elijah! I want to follow you. Let me first say goodbye to my family and friends," Elisha said.

Elijah replied, "All right, my son. Do what you have to do, but join me as soon as you can!"

Elisha said goodbye to his family and friends and made a feast for them, a feast of oxen, cooked over a fire made with Elisha's wooden yokes!

Then Elisha followed Elijah.

Discuss:
- Do you think it was easy or hard for Elisha to follow Elijah? Why?
- How do you think Elisha's family felt when he left?
- Being a follower isn't always easy. Being a leader isn't always easy either. But, whether we lead or follow, God is with us.

Prayer

Holy God, we thank you for leading us. We are proud to be your followers. Help us to follow you well. *Amen.*

Thank the children for joining you and invite them to return to their seats.

42

2 Kings 2:1-15

Suddenly a chariot of fire pulled by horses of fire came between them, and Elijah was taken up to heaven by a whirlwind.
(2 Kings 2:11b, *Today's English Version*)

Summary

In this reading from the second book of Kings, Elisha takes over the work of Elijah. In today's homily, children hear the story and discuss what is means to be both an apprentice and an heir.

Materials

Bible
a will (a real one is fine, or create a pretend document with *Last Will and Testament* printed across the top)

Homily

Invite the children to come forward and sit in a semicircle around you.

Begin the homily by discussing:
■ Imagine that you are going away and you want someone to look after your things. How would you ask them to do that?

Invite the children's responses. When the children stop offering ideas, or when someone suggests *leaving a note*, show children the will and ask:
■ Do any of you recognize this kind of note? What is it?
■ This is called a *will*. It's the note that a person leaves before he or she dies.

■ Does anyone know what a will says? What kinds of things do *you* think would be in a note like this?
■ What do we call a person who is given something by a will? *(an heir)*
■ What is an *apprentice*? (You might ask if they have seen Mickey Mouse as The Sorcerer's Apprentice in Disney's *Fantasia*.)
■ How is being an *apprentice* different than being an *heir*?
■ Which would you rather be: an *heir* or an *apprentice*? Why?
■ Today's story is about a man named Elisha. Let's hear how he was both an apprentice *and* an heir!

Hold your Bible open to the second book of Kings as you tell today's story:

Elijah the prophet had chosen Elisha to be his helper. In those days, a prophet's helper was sometimes called the prophet's son. He studied all the things the prophet did and learned to do them too.

"Elisha, one day you will have to do this work without me," the prophet explained.

"I know, father," said Elisha. "But let's not talk about that now." Elisha didn't want his teacher and friend to leave him.

43

Finally the day came, and Elijah said, "Stay here, Elisha, God is calling me to Bethel."

But Elisha didn't want to stay. "No, father, I will go with you." *And they walked together.*

Later that day Elijah said, "Stay here, Elisha, God is calling me to Jericho."

But Elisha didn't want to stay. "No, father, I will go with you." *And they walked together.*

Even later that day, Elijah said, "Stay here, Elisha, God is calling me across the Jordan."

But Elisha didn't want to stay. "No, father, I will go with you." *And they walked together.*

Some other prophets went with them and stopped a little way from the river.

When Elijah and Elisha reached the Jordan, Elijah did something amazing. He rolled up his cloak and hit the water with it. The water moved out of the way, and Elijah and Elisha walked on the dry river bed across the Jordan!

Elijah was proud of his apprentice. He knew it would be hard for Elisha to be left behind. He also knew that God was calling him somewhere Elisha was not ready to go.

So Elijah asked Elisha, "What would you like me to leave with you, my son?"

"Father Elijah, treat me like your real son. Give me your power and your blessing so that I can do all the things you can do."

Elijah thought for a moment. "That is a very difficult thing to promise, Elisha. If you see me go to heaven when God calls me, you will have what you ask. That is my will for you."

Suddenly, while they walked, a great horse and chariot appeared between them. Elijah got into the chariot.

"Stay here, Elisha, God is calling me to heaven."

Elisha cried, "No, father!" And before he could say any more, he saw the chariot carry Elijah into heaven. *And Elisha walked alone.*

He saw Elijah's cloak lying on the ground and he picked it up. He held it close. It smelled like Elijah.

When Elisha got to the river, he rolled up Elijah's cloak and hit the water with it, just as he'd seen his teacher do. The water moved and Elisha walked on the river bed across the Jordan.

When the other prophets saw that, they knew that Elisha had received a great blessing from his teacher, Elijah. *And they walked together.*

Prayer

Holy God, we thank you for people who teach us. Help us to remember to thank our teachers. *Amen.*

Thank the children for joining you and invite them to return to their seats.

■ ■ ■ ■ ■

2 Kings 4:8-37

**The boy sneezed seven times and
then opened his eyes. (2 Kings 4:35b,**
Today's English Version)

Summary

In this reading from the second book of Kings, Elisha brings a boy back to life. In today's homily, children experience getting quieter, then provide sound effects as today's story is told.

Materials

Bible
rhythm instruments: bells, blocks, etc.

Homily

Invite the children to come forward and sit in a semicircle around you.

Begin the homily by asking:
■ How many of us play instruments? Which ones?
■ How many of us read music?
■ If you read music, how do you know when to play louder and when to play more softly?
■ Today, we are all going to play instruments. Sometimes we'll play loudly; sometimes we'll play softly and quietly.
■ Whenever I put my finger in front of my lips and say, "Shhh," play more quietly.
■ Whenever I raise my hand over my head, play louder!

Distribute the rhythm instruments. Clapping hands is fine, too. Begin your musical interlude. Give the children a chance to play with more and less volume. When you are about to finish, give the "Shhh" direction several times, until the music is nearly inaudible. Stop the music by saying, simply, "the end."

Thank the children for their effort. Continue:
■ Today we practiced getting quieter and quieter because the story we're going to hear today happened in a place called Shunem (Shoo-nem) and Shunem means "a place of quiet" or "a place of rest."
■ I'll need your help to tell the story. When ever I say the word, *rest*, you make the "Shhh" sound I made when you were playing the instruments.
■ When I say the word *sneeze*, make a sneezing noise.

Hold your Bible open to the second book of Kings as you tell today's story:

A prophet named Elisha was working very hard. He needed a place to rest. *(Shhh...)*

He went to a town called Shunem. The town's name means, "a place to rest." *(Shhh...)*

A rich woman lived in Shunem. She was sure that Elisha was a man of God, so she invited him to stay at her house. She even made a guest room just for him.

Whenever he was near Shunem, he would go there to rest. *(Shhh...)*

Elisha wanted to thank the woman for being so nice. He called her to the doorway and made her a promise.

"By this time next year, you'll have a baby boy. Then you'll be the one who needs rest!" *(Shhh...)*

The woman could hardly believe Elisha, but sure enough, she had a baby the next year. The woman and her husband were very happy.

Several years later, the boy went to help his father in the fields. It was a hot day. Soon he told his father, "My head hurts!" His father had him carried home. His mother held him close. But the boy died.

His mother cried, "You are too young to be at rest!" *(Shhh...)*

The woman put the boy in Elisha's room and ran to find the prophet. When she found him, she fell at his feet and asked him to help her.

Elisha went to her house.

"I'll go to the boy and take care of everything," Elisha promised. "You stay here and rest." *(Shhh...)*

When Elisha saw the boy, he held him to help warm him up. Elisha breathed into the boy's mouth.

"Until I help you, boy, I promise I won't rest." *(Shhh...)*

Then, the boy sneezed! He sneezed, and sneezed, and sneezed...seven times!

Elijah picked him up and took the boy to his mother.

She was so happy! She hugged the boy.

"Thank you so much, Elisha!"

They had all been through a lot. So they all decided to rest. *(Shhh...)*

Prayer

God, we thank you for our lives. We want to live as your people. Show us how to help each other whenever we can. *Amen*.

Thank the children for joining you and invite them to return to their seats.

2 Kings 5:1-15

"Now why can't you just wash yourself, as he said, and be cured?"
(2 Kings 5:13b, *Today's English Version*)

Summary

In this reading from the second book of Kings, Elisha cures Naaman's disease. In today's homily, children experience doing something "the hard way" and "the easy way," then hear Naaman's story.

Materials

Bible
a jar of jelly beans

Note: *You need to know how many jelly beans are in the jar.* Raisins will work instead of jelly beans, and are a good alternative if you wish to avoid a sugary treat.

Homily

Invite the children to come forward and sit in a semicircle around you.

Begin the homily by explaining:
- I've brought a jar of jelly beans today.
- I'd like to share them with you, but first you will have to accomplish a task.
- Your task is to find out how many jelly beans there are in this jar.

Pause and place the jar in front of the children on the floor. Let them experiment to find out how many jelly beans there are.

Children might try guessing. They may also open the jar and start counting. If none of the children resort to *asking* you how many jelly beans are in the jar, which of course would be the easiest way to find out, interrupt their efforts and say:
- I can think of a *much* easier way to find out how many jelly beans there are:
- Why don't you ask me!

When the children have asked you how many jelly beans there are, tell them and ask in turn:
- How many jelly beans are there?
- That's absolutely correct!

At this point, distribute a few jelly beans to each child and continue:
- In what different ways did we try to figure out how many jelly beans there were?
- What was the *easiest* way?
- Today's story is about a man who didn't believe "the easy way" would work.

Hold your Bible open to the second book of Kings as you tell today's story:

A long time ago, there was a prophet named Elisha. God gave Elisha messages to take to the people. God gave Elisha power to make sick people well again.

Many people knew that Elisha could do those things, and they went to him when they needed help.

In a country called Syria, not far from Israel, there was a man called Naaman. Naaman was a soldier. Naaman got sick with a disease that made his skin turn white.

"I feel awful," said Naaman. "My skin looks like it's going to fall off!"

Even Naaman's friends didn't want to get too close to him. Naaman was very sad.

The king of Syria heard that there was a prophet in Israel who could heal people. The king sent Naaman to find the prophet.

When Naaman found Elisha, he said, "Please help me. I want to be well again."

"Hmm." The prophet thought a while, then said, "Naaman, you can wash off your sick skin. Go to the river Jordan and take a bath. No...take *seven* baths, and then your skin will be like new."

How do you think Naaman reacted to the idea of taking seven baths? Imagine you are Naaman, what would you say to Elisha right now?

When Naaman left Elisha's house, he was angry!

"Did you hear that?" he shouted to his servants. "He wants me to take seven baths in the Jordan River! The rivers where I live are better than the Jordan. I thought Elisha would do something for me; instead, he tells me to take baths!"

Naaman's servants talked about what had happened. Finally, one of them got up the courage to go to Naaman and say, "Sir, if the prophet had asked to do something hard, like climb a mountain or fast for a week, or make a sacrifice to God, you would have done it. Why would you rather be cured the hard way when Elisha has given you an easy way to get better? Won't you at least try what he said?"

Naaman thought about what his servant said and decided he had nothing to lose. He went to the Jordan River and bathed seven times.

The seventh time, when he came out of the water, his skin looked perfect!

Naaman went back to Elisha and thanked him.

"Now I know that you are a true prophet and your God is the true God!"

Prayer

Holy God, there are many ways for us to learn. Thank you for our teachers. Help us to help one another. *Amen.*

Thank the children for joining you and invite them to return to their seats.

■ ■ ■ ■ ■

Job

"The Lord gave, and now he has taken away. May his name be praised!" (Job 1:21b, *Today's English Version***)**

Summary

In today's story, a summary of the events of the book of Job, Job loses everything but strives to be faithful to God. In today's homily, children play a game to experience gain and loss, then hear Job's story.

Materials

Bible
small bags of popped popcorn, 1 per child
container to conceal the bags of popcorn
basket or bowl of unpopped popcorn

Homily

Invite the children to come forward and sit in a semicircle around you.

Begin the homily by explaining:
■ Today we are going to play a little game.
■ We'll all start with five kernels of unpopped popcorn.
■ I'll say something. If what I say is true *about you*, you may take a kernel of popcorn from the basket.
■ If what I say is *not* true about you, you must put a kernel of popcorn *into* the basket.

Distribute five kernels of unpopped corn to each child. Here are sample statements; make up more, if you like, to extend the game:
■ I'm wearing brown shoes.
■ I'm taller than the person on my right.
■ I've been to a doctor's office this week.
■ I have more than one brother or sister.
■ My hair is curly.
■ My toothpaste is blue.
■ I share a bedroom.
■ I've been to a movie in a theater
■ I walked to church today.
■ I have at least one middle name.

After the game, discuss:
■ Did you like the game?
■ How did you feel when you took another kernel of popcorn?
■ How did you feel when you had to put a kernel back?
■ How do you feel now?

Invite children to return the kernels to the basket or bowl. Continue:
■ In this game, did we do anything to *earn* the kernels of popcorn?
■ Did we make the things I asked about happen? For example, did we give ourselves a middle name?
■ We gained or lost kernels based on things that we can't control. We didn't deserve to gain or lose those kernels.
■ The same thing happened to a man named Job.

Pause and distribute the bags of popped corn. Here's a treat for you to eat while you listen to Job's story.

Hold your Bible open to the book of Job as you tell today's story:

Job was a rich man.

One day, he lost everything.

"God gives and God takes. Thank you, God, for everything," said Job.

Job's friends were surprised that he wasn't angry about all this.

Then Job got sick. He felt awful.

"God gives and God takes. Thank you God for everything," said Job.

Job's friends were surprised that he wasn't angry about all this.

Finally, Job wanted to talk to God.

"What is happening, God? I don't understand."

God answered Job: "Job, I'm God. Don't worry; *I* understand!"

Job was embarrassed. Even if he didn't understand, God did. That was enough for Job.

God was pleased that Job trusted him. God made Job healthy again. God gave Job more than he had before.

Job was pleased too. Whenever he thought of these things, he remembered to say:

"God gives and God takes. Thank you, God, for everything."

Ask:
- How is what happened to Job like taking the kernels of corn?
- Are we always happy with what we have?
- Maybe Job's prayer will help us remember that God always takes care of us. Let's say Job's prayer together:

Prayer

God gives and God takes. Thank you God, for everything. *Amen*.

Thank the children for joining you and invite them to return to their seats.

Isaiah 6:1-8

Then I heard the Lord say, "Whom shall I send? Who will be our messenger?" I answered, "I will go! Send me!" (Isaiah 6:8, *Today's English Version*)

Summary

In this reading from the book of Isaiah, Isaiah remembers God's call. In today's homily, children hear the story, talk about volunteering and draw pictures of what they imagine Isaiah saw when God called him.

Materials

Bible
drawing paper
markers

Homily

Invite the children to come forward and sit in a semicircle around you.

Begin the homily by distributing paper and markers.

Invite the children to listen to the story and to draw what Isaiah describes as you read the story. Pace the reading to allow the children time to hear what you say and represent it in their artwork.

Hold your Bible open to the book of Isaiah as you tell today's story:

I saw God. God was sitting on a high throne; God looked very important.

God's robe filled the whole temple.

There were two creatures standing by God.

It looked as though the clothes of each creature were made out of fire.

Each one had six wings.

Two wings covered the face. Two wings covered the body. The last two wings were for flying.

The creatures were singing a song to each other. The words were:

> **Holy, holy, holy!**
> **The Lord Almighty is Holy!**
> **God's glory fills the world!**

The sound of the song made the temple feel like it was shaking.

There was a fire burning on the altar.

The smoke filled the temple.

I was scared!

I thought, "I'm an ordinary person, but I am looking at God."

Then one of the creatures flew over to me, and the creature was carrying a coal from the fire.

The creature touched the coal to

my lips. It didn't hurt me. It made me feel good. It was no ordinary coal from an ordinary fire.

The creature said, "God forgives you; you are blessed."

Then I heard a very big voice. It was God's voice.

God said, "Whom shall I send? Who will be my messenger?"

I answered: "I will go! Send me!"

Ask:
- Who will volunteer to show us their drawings and tell us about them?
- What was the last thing that happened in Isaiah's dream?

Acknowledge the children's responses. Invite them to repeat Isaiah's words with you several time:
- I will go! Send me!

Ask:
- Has someone at your school or at your house or here at our church asked for a helper?
- Have you volunteered to be a helper?
- How did it feel to be a helper?
- How do you think Isaiah felt when he volunteered to be a helper for God?
- Everyone needs helpers from time to time. God needs helpers. Isaiah was one of God's helpers.
- You and I can be God's helpers, too.
- How can *we* be God's helpers?
- It feels good to be a helper. Let's all try to be helpers whenever we can.

Prayer

Holy God, you call us to be helpers. Please show us how to be kind to one another. Help us to help others. *Amen*.

Thank the children for joining you and invite them to return to their seats.

Isaiah 9:2-4, 6-7

The people who walked in darkness have seen a great light. They lived in a land of shadows, but now light is shining on them. (Isaiah 9:2, *Today's English Version***)**

Summary

In this reading from the book of Isaiah, the prophet uses a poem to encourage his hearers. In today's homily, children experience "shadows," hear what Isaiah said and create a closing prayer poem.

Materials

Bible
newsprint or poster board
felt marker
bed sheet
flashlight

Before the homily, copy the words of the prayer poem printed at the end of the homily on newsprint or poster board, including the blank spaces.

As the homily begins, dim the lights in the worship space, if possible.

Homily

Invite the children to come forward and sit in a semicircle around you.

Begin the homily by asking:
- Have any of you ever been in a shadow? What do you remember about it?
- Are there shadows in this room now?

- Here's a sheet. Would some of you like to get under the sheet to see what it's like to be inside a shadow?
- Please be quiet inside the shadow so you can hear the questions I'll ask you.

Pause and let the volunteers gather. Balloon the sheet over them and let it settle. Ask the children under the sheet:
- What does it look like in there?
- Do you see shadows?
- Why or why not?
- Let's see what happens if I do something else.

Turn on the flashlight and move the beam of light around the sheet's surface. Ask:
- What do you see now?
- How is it different than before?

Advise the children that you're going to remove the sheet and do so, billowing it over their heads. Continue:
- How did it feel to be in the shadow?
- How do you think it would feel to be in that shadow all the time?
- How does it feel to be in the light?
- How would it feel to be in a much brighter, warmer light, like the sun?

Hold your Bible open to the book of Isaiah as you tell today's story:

A long time ago, a prophet named Isaiah took a message from God to the people of Israel. Some of the people weren't treating others fairly. Some even stopped worshiping God.

Isaiah said to the people, "God wants you to be kind to each other! God wants you to worship again!" Isaiah warned the people that if they didn't, their lives would be hard. God was ready to punish Israel.

How do you think the people felt when Isaiah told them that they were not living God's way? *(Pause for children's responses.)*

Isaiah didn't want the people to forget that God loved them, even when God was unhappy with what they did. So God gave them a promise. It was a promise that was a poem:

> The people who walked in
>   darkness
>   have seen a great light.
> They lived in a land of shadows,
>   but now light is shining on
>   them.
>
> A child is born to us!
>   A son is given to us!
>   And he will be our ruler.
> He will be called, "Wonderful
>   Counselor,"
>   "Mighty God," "Eternal
>   Father,"
>   "Prince of Peace."

Discuss:
- ■ Have you ever heard this poem?
- ■ The poem was meant to help people have courage.
- ■ What helps you have courage?
- ■ For our closing prayer, let's create a poem that helps us have courage. I've started the poem; help me fill in the blanks. Our poem doesn't have to rhyme.

Raise the lights in the worship space as you work together to write today's closing prayer poem.

AND HIS NAME WILL BE CALLED "*wonderful counselor,* **MIGHTY GOD** everlasting father, Prince of Peace."

isaiah 9

Prayer

God, sometimes we're frightened.
Sometimes, we're sad.
Give us _____
Help us to be glad.
Let us see your light
Teach us _____
We give you thanks.
We give you _____
Guide us through all our days.
Amen.

Thank the children for joining you and invite them to return to their seats.

Isaiah 11:1-10

He will rule his people with justice and integrity. (Isaiah 11:5, *Today's English Version*)

Summary

In this reading from the book of Isaiah, the prophet's poem promises a peaceful kingdom. In today's homily, children discuss promises, hear today's story and learn the Hebrew words for *wisdom, knowledge* and *peace*.

Materials

Bible

Homily

Invite the children to come forward and sit in a semicircle around you.

Begin the homily by asking:
- What is a riddle?
- Do we know any riddles? What are they?

Invite two or three children each to share a riddle before continuing:
- I have a riddle for you.
- Think quietly about my riddle; let's give everyone a chance to think about it before we solve it.
- What do you give so you can keep it?

After the children have a moment to think about an answer, invite them to offer their ideas. Continue:
- The answer is: *a promise!*
- Have you ever made a promise?
- Has someone made a promise to you?

- How did you feel when someone promised you something?
- Today's story is about a promise. It's a promise that God made to God's people, Israel. God's promise was given to the people of Israel by a prophet named Isaiah.
- Let's hear the promise. While I tell you about it, imagine what the people who first heard it might have thought.

Hold your Bible open to the book of Isaiah as you tell today's story:

Think of King David's family and imagine it is a great tall tree. The tree got sick and was cut down. All that was left was the stump.

If a tree is cut down, is the stump alive or dead? Can a tree live without branches? Can it live without roots?

God promised:

> **New branches will grow from the tree stump. A new king will come from David's family.**

> **This king will be very special. He will have the wisdom and knowledge to be a good king. Most of all, the new king will be fair.**

> **The people will live in peace. Even animals will live in peace:**

wolves and sheep, leopards and goats, calves and lions will all live together and there won't be any fighting.

And *everyone* will know God. *Everyone!*

Discuss:
- What does God promise in our story?
- What does God promise the new king will be like?
- What would it be like to live during that king's reign?

If necessary, remind children that God promises the king will be wise, smart and fair, and that the king's people will live in peace.

Continue:
- Do any of us know a language other than English? Which languages do we know?
- What language do you imagine Isaiah spoke?
- Isaiah spoke in the Hebrew language. I'd like to teach you some words from this story in Hebrew. The words are *wisdom*, *knowledge* and *peace*:
  — "Wisdom" is *hokmah* (a guttural *h*, khawk-maw).
  — "Knowledge" is *yadah* (yaw-dah). *(You might observe that the name for the all-knowing character in the Star Wars trilogy, Yoda, is a form of this word.)*
  — "Peace" is *shalom*. The word *shalom* is often used as a greeting and a farewell; it's a way of wishing your friends a happy, healthy, whole life.

Have the children practice these words a few times. Then discuss:
- How does it feel to say a word that's so different from the ones you're used to saying?
- Isaiah was used to bringing the people warnings that God was not happy with them.
- How do you think Isaiah felt when he brought a much happier message from God than he was used to bringing?
- Isaiah took all God's messages to the people. He took warning and he took promise. Which do you think the people liked better?
- We all want to hear promises, even if they sound a little different from what we're used to hearing.
- So, we could think of God's promise as: *hokmah + yadah = shalom*. That's a promise that we might all like to add to our lives!

Prayer

Holy God, we know you promise to care for us. Give us wisdom, knowledge and peace. Help us to grow from the roots of your love. *Amen.*

Thank the children for joining you and invite them to return to their seats.

■ ■ ■ ■ ■

Isaiah 40:1-11

A voice cries out, "Prepare in the wilderness a road for the Lord! Clear the way in the desert for our God!"
(Isaiah 40:3, *Today's English Version*)

Summary

In this reading from the book of Isaiah, the prophet brings a message that the people should prepare for God. In today's homily, children build a "road," hear today's story and discuss what it means to prepare.

Materials

Bible
several toy trucks: bulldozers, back-
  hoes, dump trucks
bag of building blocks with flat,
  smooth sides

Homily

Invite the children to come forward and sit in a semicircle around you.

Begin the homily by asking:
- How many of us came to church today on a road?
- What was the road like?
- Have you ever tried to go some-where without being on a road? Where?
- What was it like getting where you wanted to go without a road?
- Today's story talks about a road. Let's listen to what it says.

Hold your Bible open to the book of Isaiah as you tell today's story:

There was a man named Isaiah who was a prophet. He listened to and told the people what God said.

One of Isaiah's messages was this:

There is a voice...do you hear it? Listen! The voice is calling from the desert. Can you hear the voice? It's far away.

There it is!

The voice is saying:

> "Get ready! God is traveling through the desert. Make a road for God! Clear the way for God!
>
> "Wherever there are low places, fill them up; wherever there are hills, knock them down.
>
> "Make the road for God smooth and flat and easy to travel.

"It will be easy for everyone to see God on that road. That's God's promise!"

Discuss:
- Have *you* ever built a road?
- What does it take to build a road?

Take the blocks from the bag and distribute them on the floor within the semicircle, piling a few in several locations and scattering the rest, so there are "hills and valleys."

Continue by saying:
- We can *talk* about building roads, or we can *build* them.
- Think about the words of the voice in today's story; what did the voice say to do with the low places and high places?
- Use the blocks to build a road.

Give the children 1-2 minutes to accomplish this task. As they work, ask them to describe what they are doing. When they are done, continue:
- Let's look at the road you built.
- Imagine that people will read about this road someday. What would you say it looks like? What would you say about building it?
- What was it like to have so many people working on our road? How important is working together?
- We worked on this road together. Working together is a great way for God's people to get where they want to go.

Prayer

Holy God, you know where we are all the time. Help us stay on the road that leads us to you. Thank you for being with us. *Amen*.

Thank the children for joining you and invite them to return to their seats.

Isaiah 45:18-19

**The Lord created the heavens—he is
the one who is God! (Isaiah 45:18a,
Today's English Version)**

Summary

In this reading from the book of
Isaiah, the prophet celebrates God's
creation in a poem. In today's homily,
children explore putting things "in
order," hear today's story and discuss
how God's creations differ from those
made by people.

Materials

Bible
bag containing several dozen inter-
locking, children's building bricks

Homily

Invite the children to come forward
and sit in a semicircle around you.

Begin the homily by dumping the
building bricks in a pile on the floor in
front of the children. Discuss:
- Imagine that this circle is our living
room. Some people are coming to
visit soon.
- What do you think we should do
with this pile of bricks?
- Shall we stack the bricks? Shall we
build something with them?

Invite the children to arrange the
bricks as they wish. Let this be a coop-
erative effort, involving as many children as possible.

Continue:
- How do you feel about straighten-
ing things up?
- How did it feel to make this struc-
ture out of a jumble of blocks?
- Is this work or play? It might be a
little of both!
- Let's listen to today's story from the
Bible. It's about building something. See if you can figure out
what it is.

Hold your Bible open to the book of
Isaiah as you tell today's story:

**God and the prophet Isaiah sang a
song. It was a kind of duet. Who
can tell me what a duet is?**

**In this duet, God sang first and
then Isaiah sang back. Here's their
song:**

**God sang,
"I am the one who made the
earth
and the people who live
on it!"**

59

God sang,
   "I am the one who used my
      strength
      to stretch the heavens from
         here to there!"

God sang,
   "I am the one who spins the
      sun
      and the moon and the stars!"

Isaiah was so amazed by what God
sang, he sang right back:

Isaiah sang,
   "God is the one who created
      the heavens!"

Isaiah sang,
   "God made the earth so that it's
      strong!"

Isaiah sang,
   "God made the earth a good
      place
      for people to live!"

Isaiah sang,
   "God tells us,
      'There is just one of me;
      I am the only God.

I've told you what I want for
   my people.
I am God and what I say
   is true!'"

Discuss:
■ What do you think of the song God
   and Isaiah sang?
■ Do you think they liked singing it?
■ Remember I said this song was
   about building something? What
   did *God* build?
■ How is what God built different
   from what people can build? Can
   people build the earth, the sky or
   the stars?
■ Building the world and making it a
   place where people can live, love
   and learn is a wonderful thing. Let's
   thank God for all these things.

Prayer

O God, thank you for making us a part
of your world. Help us care for it and
for each other. *Amen.*

Thank the children for joining you and
invite them to return to their seats.

Isaiah 52:13–53:12

"After a life of suffering, he will again have joy; he will know that he did not suffer in vain." (Isaiah 53:11a, *Today's English Version*)

Summary

In today's reading from the book of Isaiah, the prophet tells of the servant who gives his life for others. In today's homily, children talk about substituting one thing for another, then hear and discuss today's story.

Materials

Bible
small container of honey
small container of sugar

Homily

Invite the children to come forward and sit in a semicircle around you.

Begin the discussion by saying:
■ Imagine that I wanted to bake a cake. What would I need?

Hold the container of honey and ask:
■ What if the recipe called for a cup of honey but I didn't have any? What could I do? What could I use in place of the honey?
■ Yes, I could use sugar! If the recipe called for one cup of honey, I could use 3/4 cup of sugar and 1/4 cup of water instead.
■ Now imagine that I planned today's visit with you, but, at the last minute, I got sick.
■ What might happen to this time?

Acknowledge the children's responses. If necessary, mention that another person might be asked to lead the homily. Continue:
■ What do we call someone who "stands in" for another person?
■ What do you call a person who teaches your class at school on a day when your regular teacher isn't there?
■ What do both of the examples we've talked about have in common?

Acknowledge the children's responses. If necessary, explain that someone who "stands in" for another is called a "substitute." Say:
■ Today's Bible story is about a very special substitute.

Hold your Bible open to the book of Isaiah as you tell today's story:

The prophet Isaiah wrote lots of poems. Some of the poems he wrote were about a person he called God's "servant."

What is a *servant*? Who knows what a servant does? (*Allow time for children's responses before continuing:*)

Sometimes a servant has a specific job; sometimes a servant's job is to do whatever he or she is asked to do.

61

The servant Isaiah talked about had a very specific job. What he was asked to do was a very hard thing. He was asked to substitute for all the crimes, all the sins of God's people, even though he never did anything wrong. The servant was willing to take someone else's punishment.

Isaiah says:

God's servant will accept the penalty
for wrongs he did not commit.
God's servant will do this
so the people who did the wrong will be forgiven.

God's servant is very strong and very brave.
God's servant is a very special person.
He is the only one God will ever ask to do this hard job.

Because God's servant was willing to do even this job,
God will bless him.
God will make sure that the servant
knows what he did was very good.

God will make sure the people
know how much the servant did for them;
they will remember him
and honor him forever.

Isaiah's poem was about a servant whose name we never hear in the story. Does the servant remind you of any person in the Bible whose name we *do* know? *(Allow times for children's responses.)*

Many people think of *Jesus* when they hear Isaiah's poem. When you think of Jesus, does anything about Isaiah's poem sound familiar?

Jesus said that he was a servant. When he died, he paid with his life for crimes he didn't commit. He was a substitute for sinners. We remember his love for people and we honor him.

We don't know the name of the servant in Isaiah, but we know Jesus' name!

Prayer

Holy God, you sent your servant to free your people. Help us to grow and understand more about him. Thank you for your servant and for your love. *Amen*.

Thank the children for joining you and invite them to return to their seats.

Isaiah 60:1-6, 9

Look around you and see what is happening: Your people are gathering to come home! (Isaiah 60:4, *Today's English Version*)

Summary

In this reading from the book of Isaiah, the prophet celebrates his people's return to Jerusalem. In today's homily, children make pennants, discuss homecoming and celebrate with Isaiah's poem as a model.

Materials

Bible
brightly colored construction paper, cut into long triangles
masking tape
craft sticks 10" or longer
felt markers, crayons or colored pencils

Homily

Invite the children to come forward and sit in a semicircle around you.

Begin the homily by discussing:
■ Who has been to a football game?
■ What do the people who go to the game do while they are there?
■ Many schools have a big football game once a year at a time called homecoming.
■ Have any of you been to a school homecoming?
■ Who would go to a homecoming at a school?
■ At a homecoming football game, people cheer and wave banners for their team. They celebrate being the home team! They celebrate being in a place with good memories and friends again.
■ Let's celebrate a story in the Bible about a homecoming. It's a homecoming for God's people. After a long time away from the city of Jerusalem, God's people were back.
■ They didn't play football, but they did celebrate being in a place with good memories and friends again.
■ I have some things here to make pennants or banners for the homecoming. As I read the story, imagine what you might put on your banner to show that you were celebrating this homecoming.

Hold your Bible open to the book of Isaiah as you tell today's story:

The prophet Isaiah sang a song about Jerusalem. It was a happy song. God's people had been away from the city for a long time and now they were coming home.

***Arise!* Get up, Jerusalem!**

Shine like the sun! God's glory is already shining on you.

Everyone will see how wonderful it is in Jerusalem. Everyone will want to come here!

Look around. See? It's happening already. Your people are coming home!

This is a happy time. This is an exciting time!

Arise! Get up, Jerusalem.

Shine like the sun!

Hooray for God! God's people are coming home!

Ask:
- What could we put on our banners to celebrate the homecoming?
- Let's make the banners!

Distribute construction paper and felt markers, crayons or colored pencils. As the children draw, encourage their efforts.

After a minute or two, help each child tape a craft stick to his or her banner. Then continue:

- Let's stand and wave our banners.
- We can be the home team celebrating God's people coming back to Jerusalem.
- I'll lead the cheer first and then you join in:
  Leader: Arise!
  Children: Arise!
  Leader: Shine like the sun!
  Children: Shine like the sun!
  Leader: God's people are coming home!
  Children: God's people are coming home!

Prayer

Holy God, we thank you for celebrations, for good memories and for friends. Help us remember to cheer for you every day. *Amen.*

Thank the children for joining you and invite them to return to their seats.

■ ■ ■ ■ ■

Isaiah 64:1-9a

**But you are our father, Lord. We are
like clay, and you are like the potter.
(Isaiah 64:8, *Today's English Version*)**

Summary

In this reading from the book of
Isaiah, the prophet prays for God to
touch the lives of the people of faith.
In today's homily, children make a clay
vessel, then hear Isaiah's prayer.

Materials

Bible
clay
wet cloth
dry cloth
plastic container to hold the wet cloth

Homily

Invite the children to come forward
and sit in a semicircle around you.

Begin the homily by discussing:
■ Imagine that I wanted to grow
some flowers inside my house.
What would I need?
■ That's right: I would need a place
to put the dirt and the seeds and
the water. I would need a flower-
pot.
■ I don't have a flowerpot. But I do
have some clay! What could I do?
■ I have a lot of clay. Here is some for
each of you.
■ How does the clay feel now, when
you first hold it?
■ Squeeze the clay. Squish it in your
hand. Roll it between your palms.
How does it feel now?
■ There's a story about clay in the

Bible. While I tell you the story,
keep molding your clay. Shape it
however you like.

Hold your Bible open to the book of
Isaiah as you tell today's story:

**There was a prophet named
Isaiah. He listened to God and told
the people what God said. Isaiah
did that for a long time.**

**Isaiah also prayed to God for the
people:**

God, look at us!

**Here we are in this big world.
Sometimes we don't know what
to do.**

Come help us!

**You can open up the sky and
shake the mountains. If you can
do that, you can take care of us!**

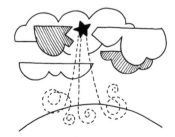

**You used to do things that really
made people notice you! Why
don't you do those things now?**

There isn't any other God, but you. We know you are our God.

Our prayer is just for you. You are happy when we pray to you.

We are like clay, God, and you are like the potter.

You made us, God!

We need you to make us into something good.

We know you can hear our prayer, God. You are listening, aren't you?

Discuss:
- What do you think Isaiah meant when he said we are like clay?
- What do you think Isaiah meant when he said God is like the potter?
- Can clay do anything by itself?
- What could a potter do without clay?

Invite volunteers to show you what they have done with their clay.
Discuss:
- Look at what you make with your clay. Look very closely. What do you see? Do you see fingerprints?
- Do you know that your fingerprints are different from everyone else's? No two people have the same fingerprints. Even identical twins have different fingerprints!

- What you make with the clay has your fingerprints. It has your special, one-of-a-kind mark on it.
- We are the clay. God is the potter.
- God made us. We have God's fingerprints on us. That's pretty special.
- Look at what you made with your clay. Look at what someone else made.
  — How are they alike?
  — How are they different?
  — They are all made of clay, but each one is special, partly because you made it!
- Now look at the person sitting next to you.
  — How are you like that person?
  — How are you different?
  — You are all people but each one of you is special, partly because God made you!
- God loves us and God's house has a special place for each of us.

Prayer

Holy God, you are the one who made us. Help us love each other the way you love us. Hear us when we pray. *Amen*.

Remind the children to take their clay creations home with them. Offer the towels to help clean fingers if necessary.

Thank the children for joining you and invite them to return to their seats.

Jeremiah 1:4-10

"I chose you before I gave you life, and before you were born I selected you to be a prophet to the nations." (Jeremiah 1:5, *Today's English Version*)

Summary

In this reading from the book of Jeremiah, God calls the prophet to speak for God. In today's homily, children hear and discuss this story, then plant seeds to remind them that they, too, are growing.

Materials

Bible
small flowerpots or other containers filled with soil, 1 per child (plastic cups work nicely)
seeds (flower or vegetable)
damp towel
dry towel
plastic bag or bowl for the damp towel

Homily

Invite the children to come forward and sit in a semicircle around you.

Begin the homily by discussing:
- Today we're going to hear a story about a young man. His name was Jeremiah. God called Jeremiah to be a prophet.
- What is a *prophet*? Who knows what a prophet does?
- That's right, a prophet tells God's message to God's people.

- When God called Jeremiah to be a prophet, Jeremiah thought of several reasons why he shouldn't take the job.
- Here's Jeremiah's story.

Hold your Bible open to the book of Jeremiah as you tell today's story:

God said to me, "Jeremiah, I chose you to be a prophet before you were even born!"

I said, "God, I'm too young. I don't know what to say."

"Don't say you're too young, Jeremiah. Go tell my people what I say. I'll take care of you."

Then God reached out and touched my lips and said, "Here, Jeremiah. Here are the words you need. You'll be a great prophet!"

Discuss:
- When did God decide that Jeremiah should be a prophet?
- How would God know what Jeremiah would be before he was even born?

Acknowledge the children's responses and continue:
- God knows everything.

- Sometimes even *we* know what something will become before it grows up.
- Here are some flowerpots *(or cups)* and some seeds. Do we know what these seeds will become if we plant them?
- If we plant *sunflower* seeds, we'll get *sunflowers*! If we plant *tomato seeds*, we'll get *tomatoes*! What happens if we plant *carrot* seeds? *petunia* seeds? *squash* seeds?

Distribute the seeds and flowerpots or cups. If you are using only one flowerpot for the homily, distribute the seeds and invite the children to move closer to the flowerpot.

Plant the seeds. The children can use a finger to poke a hole or two into the soil, then drop in a few seeds and cover them. Suggest the children water these when they get home, or, if you wish, keep the seeds at church and arrange for them to be cared for during the week.

Use the towels to clean hands. Conclude:
- God called Jeremiah to be a prophet. Jeremiah didn't know what he'd be when he grew up, but God did!
- We are all God's children. God calls each of us, too. Like Jeremiah, God calls us to tell others about God's love.
- These plants will remind us that God has already planted the seeds of what we will be inside of us. We may not know what we'll do when we grow up, but God does.
- And we're already growing!

Prayer

God, you plant your seeds in us. Help us to grow to be strong. Thank you for calling us to be your people. *Amen*.

Thank the children for joining you and invite them to return to their seats.

Jeremiah 17:5-10

"I will bless the person who puts his trust in me." (Jeremiah 17:7, *Today's English Version*)

Summary

In this reading from the book of Jeremiah, the prophet hears God's promise to bless those who trust in God. In today's homily, children take a brief "trust walk," then hear God's promise in today's story.

Materials

Bible
several stuffed animals

Homily

Invite the children to come forward and *stand* in a semicircle around you.

Begin the homily by discussing:
- Imagine I wanted to go somewhere but I couldn't see.
- How would I get to where I wanted to go?
- What would it be like to have someone take you somewhere if you couldn't see where you were going?
- Today we're going to find out what it's like to trust someone. We're going to take a trust walk.
- Pick a partner. The taller partner will be the leader first.
- We're going to walk around in this area at the front of the church.
- Do you see my stuffed animals? I'm going to place them on the floor somewhere.
- Leaders, you will have to help your partner walk around the stuffed animals. You can guide your partner with your hand and with your voice. Use a quiet voice, please!
- Followers, you will have to trust your partner. You can ask questions about where you are, but keep your eyes closed.
- Leaders, take your partner's hand. Followers, close your eyes. Ready? Start walking!

Place the stuffed animals on the floor in several spots. After a minute, have the children switch roles. Rearrange the stuffed animals.

When everyone has had a chance to lead and to follow, invite the children to sit in a semicircle around you.

Ask:
- How did you feel when you were the leader?
- How did you feel when you were the follower?
- Which was harder? Why?

Hold your Bible open to the book of Jeremiah as you tell today's story:

A prophet named Jeremiah heard something about trusting and following God:

> **When a person doesn't trust God,**
>   **that person is like a bush in the desert.**

69

When a person *does* trust God,
that person is like a tree
planted near a stream.
Which do you think is happier:
the bush or the tree?

"I'm God
and I know what people think
and how people feel.
People who trust me
feel like the tree by the
stream.
They feel safe
and they are happy with the
blessings I give them.

"People who don't trust me feel
like the bush in the desert.
They never know how they
are going to get by.

They worry and are scared.
They never feel they have
enough."

God wants people to trust
that God will take care of
them.
God is a leader who can always
keep us safe
even when things seem scary.

Discuss:
- When you were walking with your eyes closed, how did you find out where you were?
- Did anyone ask?
- Sometimes people feel lost, like they don't really see where they are even if their eyes are open. If that happens to you, ask someone for help.
- How do we ask God for help?

Prayer

God, we thank you for leading us. Show us how to follow you. We trust you to take care of us. Help us to take care of each other too. *Amen*.

Thank the children for joining you and invite them to return to their seats.

Jeremiah 31:31-34

"I will put my law within them and write it on their hearts. I will be their God and they will be my people." (Jeremiah 31:33b, *Today's English Version*)

Summary

In this reading from the book of Jeremiah, God promises a new covenant with Israel. In today's homily, children first hear the story, then decorate covenant-hearts of their own.

Materials

Bible
a contract, real or pretend
heart-shaped paper covenants, 1 per child (see **before the homily** note, below)
colored felt markers, crayons or pencils
a stamp-pad (vegetable-based, washable ink)
damp towels
dry towels

Before the homily prepare large, paper covenant-hearts, one for each child. Cut large hearts from red or pink construction paper. On each heart write:
■ I will be your God;
              will be my child.

Homily

Invite the children to come forward and sit in a semicircle around you.

Begin by introducing the Bible story:
■ Today's story from the Bible has to do with God and people making a covenant.
■ Is *covenant* a new word for us? What is a *covenant*?
■ What other words could we use instead of the word *covenant*? *(contract, promise, agreement, bargain, pact, treaty, etc.)*

Show children the real or pretend contract. Explain:
■ This is a covenant. It's a contract between two people. It clearly states says what each person promises to do for the other person.
■ A contract is really a promise in writing.
■ When our moms and dads want to remember things, do they sometimes write them down? I do. Do you?
■ Writing important things down makes them easier to remember.
■ Let's hear about a covenant that God promised to write.

Hold your Bible open to the book of Jeremiah as you tell today's story:

God said to a prophet named Jeremiah:

71

"It's about time I made a new covenant with my people. It's not going to be like the old covenant.

"The old covenant was a good one. I made that one a long time ago, when Moses was leading the people. Even though I loved my people and kept my promises, they didn't remember their part of the contract.

"I'll write the new covenant *inside* the people. It will be something they think about and remember all the time.

"It will be like I have written the contract on each of their hearts. That way, they will never forget that I am their God and they are my people."

Distribute the paper hearts and make available the felt markers, crayons or colored pencils. Explain:
■ God promises to love and care for us too, just like God promised to care for God's people, long ago.
■ Here is a covenant-heart for each of you. Make your covenant special, because you are special!

Show children how to place their names in the blank space on their covenant-hearts. Assist smaller children as necessary. Children may also decorate their hearts. While they complete the task, continue:
■ There is one more thing that people do with a covenant that we haven't mentioned yet.
■ What has to happen to make the covenant legal? What is the last step in making a contract?
■ Signing the contract!
■ Your name is one way of signing something, but today we're going to sign another way too.
■ When you finish preparing your covenant-heart, I'll help you put your fingerprint on it.

Assist each child in making a fingerprint on his or her covenant-heart. Keep the towels close by to wipe fingers clean.

When the children have all "signed" their hearts, pray together.

Prayer

O God, we know that you love us. Fill our hearts with love for each other. Help us to remember that you are our God and we are your children. *Amen*.

Thank the children for joining you and invite them to return to their seats. Remind them to keep their covenant-hearts with them as a reminder that they are all God's children.

Ezekiel 34:11-17

"I, the Sovereign Lord, tell you that I myself will look for my sheep and take care of them.." (Ezekiel 34:11, *Today's English Version***)**

Summary

In this reading from the book of the prophet Ezekiel, God promises to bring the people back into the "fold." In today's homily, children search for pieces of a puzzle, assemble the puzzle and hear the shepherd's story from Ezekiel.

Materials

Bible

children's puzzle, 25-30 pieces, preferably one picturing a familiar Bible story

Before the homily scatter some of the puzzle pieces (about 1/3) around the worship space in places the children will easily be able to find them.

Homily

Invite the children to come forward and sit in a semicircle around you.

Begin the homily by showing children the remaining pieces of the puzzle and asking:

■ What do I have here? What are these?

■ I'd like to see what this puzzle looks like. What do I need to do?

■ Let's put this puzzle together.

Work together to assemble the puzzle. If no one notices that pieces are missing, ask:

■ Is something missing here?

■ Have you ever lost something?

■ Did you know where to start looking?

■ How did you feel when you were looking?

■ How did you feel when you found what you'd lost?

■ It looks like I've lost some things, doesn't it? Maybe we can find them! Look around this area *(specify where)* for the lost pieces of the puzzle.

Let children retrieve the missing pieces and finish the puzzle. Ask:

■ What picture do we see now that all the pieces are together?

■ How did you feel when you knew the puzzle was missing some pieces?

■ Those of you who found a puzzle piece, how did you feel when you found it?

■ How did you feel when the puzzle was put together?

■ Today's Bible story is about God finding and bringing together something that is lost. Let's listen to see what that is.

Hold your Bible open to the book of Ezekiel as you tell today's story:

A long time ago, God asked a man named Ezekiel to be a messenger for God. It wasn't always easy to be God's messenger. A person had to have a strong faith.

God knew Ezekiel was right for the job. Ezekiel's name means, "God makes strong."

Sometimes God talked to Ezekiel. Sometimes Ezekiel had dreams and saw God's messages.

God told Ezekiel:

My people are like sheep. They have gone to many different places. Some of them are lost.

I am like a shepherd. I will go and find my sheep and bring them back home.

They will have enough food and water; they will have places for rest and shelter.

I will take care of them and they will be strong and safe forever."

Sheep aren't very good at finding their way back home sometimes. Sheep need a shepherd to make sure they have what they need.

God is a good shepherd. God will always know where to find you and me. God will always love us.

Prayer

God, you are a good shepherd. Help us to stay close to you and follow you. We thank you for keeping us in your love. *Amen*.

Thank the children for joining you and invite them to return to their seats.

74

Daniel 1:1-16

"Test us for ten days," he said. "Give us vegetables to eat and water to drink. Then compare us with the young men who are eating the food of the royal court, and base your decision on how we look." (Daniel 1:12-13, *Today's English Version*)

Summary

In this reading from Daniel, Daniel and his friends choose to obey God's law instead of the king's. In today's homily, children compare things based on appearance and real value, then hear today's story.

Materials

Bible
pie tin filled with shaving cream
carrot sticks

Homily

Invite the children to come forward and sit in a semicircle around you.

Begin the homily by discussing:
- Do you ever wish we had snack time in church?
- What kinds of snacks do you like?
- Today I brought a pie and some carrot sticks.
  - Which would you rather have?
  - Why?
- What do you think is good about the pie?
  - What might *not* be so good about the pie?

- What might happen if we ate a lot of pie?
- What do you think is good about the carrot sticks?
  - What might *not* be good about them?
  - What might happen if we ate a lot of carrots?
- Taking care of our bodies is important. Our bodies are a gift from God. It's fine to have treats once in a while, but we have to give our bodies the fuel they need to keep us healthy!

Explain to the children that the pie is really shaving cream. Let children smell the pie. Continue:
- How does the pie look to you now? Would you still want to eat it?
- Something that looks good might not really be very good for you.
- Would you like to have a carrot stick?

Distribute carrot sticks. Hold your Bible open to the book of Daniel as you tell today's story:

A long time ago, there was a young man named Daniel. Daniel had three best friends, Hananiah, Mishael and Azariah.

75

Daniel's people, Israel, had been invaded by the Babylonians. Daniel and his friends were taken from their home to Babylonia and sent to the court of the king to be servants there.

The king wanted his servants to eat well, so they'd be healthy. The food in the king's court included things that Jews like Daniel and his friends weren't supposed to eat.

Daniel went to the chief of the king's household and said, "My friends and I have special rules about what we eat. The rules are from God. We can't eat many of the things from the king's kitchen. Please, let us eat what God says we should."

Ashpenaz, the chief of the household, understood Daniel's problem. But he had a problem, too!

Ashpenaz said, "The king wants all the servants here to be well-fed and healthy. If you don't eat, you'll get sick and weak and the king will blame me!"

Daniel made a deal with Ashpenaz: "Let us eat vegetables and drink water for ten days. Then you can see for yourself if we are healthy or not."

Ashpenaz agreed. Ten days later, he did see for himself: Daniel and his friends were stronger and healthier than the servants who ate the same food as the king!

From that day on, Daniel and his friends ate what God's laws said instead of what the king of Babylonia said.

Ask:
- Why did Daniel and his friends want to eat vegetables?
- It would have been easier for Daniel and his friends to eat the king's food. Is the easiest thing always the best thing?
- Can you think of other times when the easiest way is not the best way?

Prayer

Holy God, you know what is good. Help us to remember to take good care of our bodies and our minds. Thank you for all your blessings. *Amen.*

Thank the children for joining you and invite them to return to their seats.

Daniel 6:1-28

"He saves and rescues; he performs wonders and miracles in heaven and on earth." (Daniel 6:27a, *Today's English Version*)

Summary

In this reading from the book of Daniel, God saves Daniel from death in the lion pit. In today's homily, children play a game of Darius Says, talk about rules and hear today's story.

Materials

Bible

Homily

Invite the children to come forward and *stand* in a semicircle around you.

Begin the homily by discussing:
- How many of you have played the game Simon Says?
- Today we're going to play a little different version of Simon Says. It's called *Darius Says*. This area, where we play the game, is *Darius's court*.
- I'll be Darius. If Darius catches you breaking the rules, you have to sit in the *lion's pit. (Indicate a nearby area as the* lion's pit.*)*
- There is one more thing that's different in this game. The game of Darius Says includes a *guardian angel.* I'll need one of you to be the *guardian angel.*

You might ask the child with the most recent birthday to be the *guardian angel.*

Continue:
- The *guardian angel* can rescue us from the *lion's pit.* If the guardian angel taps you on the shoulder, you can come out of the *lion's pit* and rejoin us in *Darius's court.*
- Does anyone have a question about how we're going to play? *Guardian angel*, remember that you can rescue the people who end up in the *lion pit.*

Play the game for several minutes, then invite the children to be seated. Hold your Bible open to the book of Daniel as you tell today's story:

A long time ago, there was a great king named Darius. He was king of the Medes, and very powerful.

Darius appointed many people to help him rule his kingdom. Darius called those people governors. One of the people Darius chose to be a governor was a young Jew named Daniel.

Daniel did such a good job that Darius was thinking about putting him in charge of all the other governors. That idea made some of the other governors jealous. They tried to think of a way to make Daniel look bad, so Darius wouldn't put him in charge. But Daniel was a good man, and the

jealous governors couldn't find anything bad to say about him. So they came up with another plan.

The jealous governors went to see Darius. "Darius," they said, "you are a great king! We think that for the next month, everyone in your kingdom should ask you for everything. No one should ask another person or even God for anything.

"Everyone will see what a great king you are. Make this a rule, Darius. If anyone breaks the rule, throw him in the lion pit!"

King Darius made the rule. The jealous governors were happy. They knew that Daniel prayed to God every day, and that he would break Darius's rule.

When Daniel heard about the rule, he went to his room, and prayed to God like he did every day, in front of his open window.

The jealous governors saw Daniel praying and went to Darius. "Daniel has broken your rule, King Darius! We saw him praying to his God. Throw him in the lion pit."

Darius liked and respected Daniel. All day, he tried to think of a way not to have to send Daniel to the lion pit, but he couldn't think of a way to save him.

That night, Daniel was thrown into the lion pit. The next morning, Darius went to the lion pit and called to Daniel. "Daniel! Daniel! You are loyal to your God; has your God saved you?"

Daniel called back to Darius. "Great King Darius, God has saved me! God sent a guardian angel to close the lions' mouths because God knew that I didn't do anything wrong."

Darius was very happy. He helped Daniel out of the lion pit.

Later, Darius made this rule: "Everyone in my kingdom will respect Daniel's God. Daniel's God rescues people and works miracles in heaven and on earth!"

Ask:
- Did Daniel break King Darius's rule? According to the king's rule, should Daniel have been thrown into the lion pit?
- Was Darius's rule a good rule?
- Was Daniel's reason for breaking the rule a good reason?
- Should people *always* be punished for breaking a rule?
- What might be a good reason to break a rule?
- What are some rules that we should *never* break?
- Remember that God knows the reasons for what we do. God wants us to obey rules. God also forgives us if we break them. We can forgive each other too.

Prayer

Holy God, you do wonderful things. Help us to obey rules. Help us to forgive each other the way you forgive us. *Amen.*

Thank the children for joining you and invite them to return to their seats.

Hosea 5:15–6:6

"I would rather have my people know me than have them burn offerings to me." (Hosea 6:6b, *Today's English Version*)

Summary

In this reading from the book of Hosea, the prophet hears God's plea for real love and not empty ritual. In today's homily, children make valentines for God, then hear and discuss today's story.

Materials

Bible
valentine hearts (see **before the session** note, below)
colored felt markers, crayons or colored pencils
large sheet of posterboard
cellophane tape

Before the session prepare valentines for each child. For each valentine, cut a heart (about 6" top to bottom) out of red or pink construction paper. On each heart write:
■ To God, from _____.

Homily

Invite the children to come forward and sit in a semicircle around you.

Begin the homily by discussing:
■ Today, we're going to make a valentine for God.
■ What is a valentine?
　— What does a valentine usually say?
　— What does a valentine usually mean?
　— When do people give valentines?
■ When is Valentine's Day?
■ Is Valentine's Day the only time a person could give or receive a valentine?

Distribute the construction paper hearts and markers, crayons or colored pencils. Invite the children to write their names in the blanks on the valentines and to continue decorating their hearts while you tell today's story.

Hold your Bible open to the book of Hosea as you begin:

A long time ago, there was a prophet named Hosea. He lived and worked in Israel.

Israel's people had forgotten the covenant—the promises—they had made with God.

God's covenant with Israel was like a marriage. Now, it wasn't exactly the same as a marriage between two people, but the idea was that God really loved Israel.

Pause to discuss:
■ Why do people get married?
■ Marriage is not the only way that people make a commitment to one

79

another. What are some other ways people commit themselves—or promise—that they will be there for each other?

■ What about joining a club or a team or a church? Members of a group are there for each other too. They choose to be together.

Continue with the story:

This is what God told Hosea:

"I love my people. I've done all the things I promised when we made our covenant, but my people have forgotten me.

"What am I going to do with them? One minute they say they will be faithful and the next minute they don't even remember that I'm here.

"Hosea, I've sent you to give them this special message:

> **I don't care about all the things you do to *act* like you remember me; I want you to really *care* about me! I don't want you to come to me just when you are in trouble; I want you to be my people all the time.**
>
> **I choose you as my people. I want you to remember that you chose me as your God!**

Discuss:
■ Wouldn't it be nice to get a valentine every day—to hear and to say, "I love you; I care about you" *every day*?
■ God loves us and cares about us *every day*. We can find a valentine from God in the Bible if we open it and read it or hear it.
■ Let's make our valentines for God!

Help the children to tape their valentine hearts on the posterboard in a large heart-shape. Write *Our Valentine to God* in big letters in the open space in the middle of the heart.

Prayer

Holy God, we are your people. Thank you for loving us. Help us to love each other and to show our love every day. *Amen.*

Thank the children for joining you and invite them to return to their seats.

If possible, display the completed poster in a public part of your church building.

Joel 2:21-27

*"Be glad, people of Zion, rejoice at what
the Lord your God has done for you."*
(Joel 2:23a, *Today's English Version*)

Summary

In this reading from the book of Joel, God promises the people a return to fullness and blessing. In today's homily, children participate in a roleplay of the story.

Materials

Bible
real or artificial flowers
real or artificial fruit
several stuffed animals
large "raindrops" cut from blue construction paper
large "grain" cut from yellow construction paper

Homily

Invite the children to come forward and sit in a semicircle around you.

Begin the homily by discussing:
- Tell me about a happy time in your life.
- Would you like to have that happy time happen again?
- If you tried to have that happy time again, how might it be the same? How might it be different?

Hold your Bible open to the book of Joel as you tell today's story:

Once upon a time, Israel was a country that had everything. There was no war. They had plenty to eat. There was enough food. God felt pleased with the people. The people felt happy with God.

The people were so happy that they started to take God and all the blessings they had for granted.

Then times got hard. There wasn't enough rain for the crops to grow. Other nations wanted to take their land.

God sent prophets to the people. The prophets scolded the people for forgetting about God. "Come back to God," they said. "God has done so much for you; why have you have forgotten God!"

God wasn't happy with the people. The people weren't happy with God.

God sent a prophet named Joel to Israel. Joel understood why the people were sad. God talked to Joel and told him that things would get better for Israel. Joel told the people what God said.

Pause in the story and distribute to each child one of the items that represent flowers, fruit, animals, rain and grain. Say:
- When I talk about the item you are holding, wave it above your heads in celebration.

■ When I talk about the people, everyone wave your hands.

Here is what God told Joel:

> **Fields, don't be afraid!**
> **Be glad, God will make you grow again.**
> **Animals, don't be afraid!**
> **Be glad, God will take care of you.**
> **Fruit will grow on the trees and there will be plenty of food for everyone.**

> **People, be glad**
> **because I am your God!**
> **I've give you just the right amount of rain;**
> **I'll give you the right amount of grain.**
> **I'll give you back everything you ever lost and more.**
> **You will know that I am your God**
> **and you will be happy again!**
> **You will praise me,**
> **and I will be happy again!**
> **Everything will be even better than the best time you remember.**

> **People, be glad**
> **because I am your God!**

Discuss:
■ Do we *always* have happy times?
■ Do we *always* get what we want?
■ It's nice to remember happy times.
■ In hard times, it's nice to believe that even better things will happen in the future.
■ We call this *hope*. Hope is a blessing that helps us get through hard times.

Prayer

God, you are the God of hope. Thank you for all the good things we remember. We know you care for us and make even better things possible. Help us to share hope with each other. *Amen*.

Thank the children for joining you and invite them to return to their seats.

Amos 7:7-15

"I had another vision from the Lord. In it I saw him standing beside a wall that had been built with a plumb line, and there was a plumb line in his hand."
(Amos 7:7, *Today's English Version*)

Summary

In this reading from the book of Amos, the prophet sees God using a plumb line to measure Israel's "uprightness." In today's homily, children use a plumb line, then hear today's story.

Materials

Bible
plumb line (To improvise, use a 4'-5' length of string with a heavy metal washer or other weight tied to one end.)
yardstick

Before the homily practice with the plumb line. Find something in the worship space that is warped, angled or "out of plumb" to show children that the plumb line really does work. Or, if everything in the worship area appears to be plumb, practice using the yardstick, holding it at an angle to demonstrate how the plumb line shows that the yardstick is not straight up and down.

Homily

Invite the children to come forward and *stand* in a semicircle around you.

Show the children the plumb line and ask:

■ What is this?
■ Who can tell me what this does?
■ Who do you think would use this? Why?
■ This is a very simple but important tool. It's called a *plumb line*. Builders use it to check and make sure that a wall is straight.
■ What could happen if a wall wasn't straight?
■ How would a builder use a plumb line? How would it tell the builder if the wall was straight or not?
■ Let's see if the walls in our worship area are straight.

At a nearby wall, continue:
■ Does this wall look straight?
■ Let's look at the wall from the side, not straight at the wall from in front.

Hold the plumb line about an inch in front of the wall at the height of your shoulders. Continue:
■ Is the string the same distance from the wall all the way down? Does the wall look straight now?

Use the yardstick to measure the distance from the wall to the string at both the top and the bottom of the string. Test one or two walls. You might also check the pulpit or lectern and one of the pews.

83

Return to the story area and invite the children to sit in a semicircle around you.

Hold your Bible open to the book of Amos as you tell today's story:

A long time ago, God sent a prophet named Amos to Israel. Amos heard God speak to him. Amos also saw things that God showed him, things that were like a dream.

Amos saw God standing next to a wall. God was holding a plumb line.

God asked, "Amos, what do you see?"

Amos said, "A plumb line."

God said, "This wall is like my people, Israel. Look! When I hold up the plumb line, you can see for yourself that my people are out of line."

Amos looked at the wall. Amos looked at the plumb line. God was right. The wall was out of line. The people were out of line!

God said, "A crooked wall is dangerous, Amos. I'm going to let it fall."

When Amos told the people what he had seen, they were angry with him. They didn't like hearing that they didn't stand up very well in front of God. They didn't want to hear that they were headed for a fall.

Some people even thought Amos was making up the whole story.

Amos told them, "Being a prophet is not my choice. I'm a farmer!

"God sent me here to warn you about the wall. It's ready to fall down. If you don't want to listen to me, you're the ones who will have to pick up the pieces."

The people didn't listen to Amos. Israel did fall. It was a long time before Israel was upright and strong again.

Prayer

Holy God, you see things the way they really are. Build our faith in you. Show us how to be true and strong, so we can stand for you. *Amen*.

Thank the children for joining you and invite them to return to their seats.

84

Jonah 1:1–2:10

**"I worship the Lord, the God of
heaven, who made land and sea."
(Jonah 1:9b, *Today's English Version*)**

Summary

In this reading from the book of
Jonah, the prophet tries to run from
God and ends up caught by a fish. In
today's homily, children talk about run-
ning away, hear today's story and create a prayer from "inside the great
fish."

Materials

Bible
small suitcase
copy of Margaret Wise Brown's *The
    Runaway Bunny* (New York:
    Harper and Row, 1942)
posterboard or newsprint
colored felt markers

Homily

Invite the children to come forward
and sit in a semicircle around you.

Begin the homily by placing the suitcase in the center of the semicircle
and asking:
- What is this?
- What do you think of when you see
  a suitcase?
- Why do people pack things and
  leave home?
- Have you heard stories about run-
  ning away from home? What stories
  have you heard?
- I have a story here that you may
  have heard before. Do you know
  this story?

Read aloud *The Runaway Bunny*.
Show children (and church members!)
the illustrations as you read.

Ask:
- What happened every time the
  little bunny thought of a new way
  to run away and hide from his
  mother?
- Why do you think the mother was
  willing to become all those things?
- The bunny reminds me of a story in
  the Bible. It's about a man named
  Jonah who wanted to run away
  from God, but everywhere Jonah
  went, God was there!

Hold your Bible open to the book of
Jonah as you tell today's story:

**Once upon a time, a very long
time ago, a man named Jonah
heard God's voice.**

**God said, "Jonah, I want you to go
to the great city called Nineveh."**

**"The people there are not living
the way they should. They cheat
each other, they don't worship
me, and they fight a lot.**

**"I want them to stop. I want them
to live in peace and to be good to
each other. You go tell them that
for me."**

**Jonah thought about this for a
while. He was scared! Nineveh was**

85

a great city, and it was a long way away!

The people wouldn't know him; why would they listen to him? What if they got mad and threw him in jail or hurt him?

'No way," thought Jonah, "I'm going in the other direction...and fast!"

Jonah got on a ship headed for Spain.

God saw Jonah and decided to bring him back. God wanted Jonah to go to Nineveh!

What do you think God did to get Jonah off that ship? *(Pause for children's responses.)*

God sent a huge wind storm! The wind blew so hard that the ship was about to break apart. The sailors threw the cargo overboard and they prayed to many gods for help.

The captain found Jonah sleeping through the whole thing. When the sailors asked Jonah who he was and why he was traveling, they knew the storm was because God was trying to get Jonah off that boat. "What should we do?" they cried.

Jonah knew. "Throw me off the boat and into the sea. The storm will stop."

The sailors didn't want to throw Jonah overboard. They tried and tried to row out of the storm, but they couldn't. Finally, they prayed and asked God to forgive them for what they were going to do. Then they threw Jonah into the sea.

The storm stopped.

Do you know what happened next? *(Invite responses.)*

That's right, God saved Jonah. God wanted Jonah to go to Nineveh! A great fish swallowed Jonah. For three days—can you imagine?— for three days Jonah lived inside the fish. People catch fish all the time, but this time the fish caught a person!

Deep inside the fish, Jonah prayed. God heard Jonah's prayer. God had the fish spit Jonah out onto the beach.

God wanted Jonah to go to Nineveh. And this time, Jonah went!

Discuss:
- What do you think it was like inside that fish?
- Let's imagine that we are Jonah and we are inside the great fish. What would we say to God?

Write the key words of children's responses on poster board or newsprint. Incorporate these ideas into today's closing prayer.

Prayer

Holy God, when we are deep inside a scary place, or when we feel alone, help us remember that you are there too. *(Add children's suggestions.)* Thank you for loving us. *Amen*.

Thank the children for joining you and invite them to return to their seats.

Micah 6:1-8

"What shall I bring to the Lord, the God of heaven, when I come to worship him?" (Micah 6:6a, *Today's English Version*)

Summary

In this reading from the book of Micah, the prophet listens to God present a legal case against Israel. In today's homily, children hear today's story, then act out the story in a "mock court."

Materials

Bible
scarf
child's choir robe (to improvise, use a large adult shirt)
small gavel or hammer (to improvise, use a wooden, child's block)

Homily

Invite the children to come forward and sit in a semicircle around you.

Begin the homily by discussing:
- ◼ Imagine that I had a complaint—there was something I didn't like. Let's say I bought a car and it wouldn't run.
- ◼ What could I do?
- ◼ What if I talked to the person who sold me the car...and the owner of the car store...and the president of the car company, and none of them would fix the car or give me my money back. What could I do then?
- ◼ Well, I could take them to court.
  - — What is a court?
  - — What happens there?
  - — Who are the people I'd see in a courtroom?
- ◼ Does God ever go to court?
- ◼ In today's story, that's just what happens.

Hold your Bible open to the book of Micah as you tell today's story:

A long time ago, God make an agreement with the people of Israel. The agreement was called a covenant.

The covenant said, "I will be your God and you will follow my rules." The rules were given to Moses, and Moses gave them to the people. Everybody agreed that this would be their covenant.

What do we call the ten rules that were an important part of the covenant? That's right, the Ten Commandments!

At first, everything went well. But as time passed, the people forgot some of what they promised. Then they forgot a little more, and a little more.

Finally, God decided to complain.

God told Micah the prophet that there would be a court case. The

court wasn't like any other court. The mountains were the jury; all of creation witnessed the agreement and heard what God had to say.

"Listen to my complaint," said God. "Sky and rocks and trees, you were here when we made our covenant. The people forgot what I want from them.

"I want them to do three things: I want them to do what they promise; I want them to treat each other with kindness; I want them to worship me because they love me and I love them."

Discuss:
■ Does that sound like what you imagine a court would be like?
■ Would anyone here like to be the judge at that court?

Choose a volunteer and outfit the *judge* with the robe and gavel. Continue:
■ Who would like to be Micah and present God's complaint?

Choose a volunteer and outfit *Micah* with the scarf over his or her shoulders. Recruit two or three other children to help *Micah*. Continue:
■ The rest of us will be the *mountain-jury*.
■ Stand up, *mountains*—you are *very* tall!
■ *Micah*, what was bothering God? Tell the *judge*!

If necessary, remind *Micah* and his or her helpers that the people of Israel have broken their agreement with God. They don't live by God's law, the Ten Commandments.

After God's case has been presented, ask the *mountain-jury*:
■ What do you think of the evidence?
■ Is Israel innocent or guilty?

Acknowledge the verdict and continue:
■ *Judge*, what does God want now?

If necessary, remind the *judge* that God wants the people to obey the Ten Commandments, to do what they promised, to treat each other kindly, to love God as God loves them, etc.

Close by saying:
■ I think God had a good case.
■ God didn't want to punish the people for forgetting the covenant.
■ God just wanted the people to remember what they promised, to be kind to each other and to love God.
■ That's something we can all try to do!

Prayer

Holy God, thank you for calling us to be your people. Help us to keep our promises, to be kind to each other and to love you always. *Amen*.

Collect the props, thank the children for joining you and invite them to return to their seats.

Habakkuk 3:17-19

"I will still be joyful and glad, because the Lord God is my savior." (Habakkuk 3:18, *Today's English Version*)

Summary

In this reading from the book of Habakkuk, the prophet sings a prayer of celebration and thanksgiving. In today's homily, children have a "when things look bad, we can still be glad" party, then hear today' story.

Materials

Bible
colored construction paper
masking tape
colored felt markers, crayons or
   colored pencils
rhythm instruments
animal crackers, 2 per child

Homily

Invite the children to come forward and sit in a semicircle around you.

Begin the homily by discussing:
- Why do people celebrate?
- What kinds of things do people celebrate?
- What are some reasons to have a party?
- Today we are going to celebrate. We're going to have a "when things look bad, we can still be glad" party.
- Is it all right to have a party when things look bad? Maybe that's when we need a party most!
- What do we need for a party?

Acknowledge the children's responses. Focus on decorations, music and food.

Distribute the construction paper and markers, crayons or pencils. Invite children to create party hats and badges to wear and posters to display while you tell them about a time in the Bible when someone wanted to have a "when things are bad, we can still be glad" celebration.

Hold your Bible open to the book of Habakkuk as you tell today's story:

A long time ago, there lived a man named Habakkuk. I've never heard of anyone else named Habakkuk, have you?

Habakkuk's name means "hug." Habakkuk was the kind of man who liked to hold on to things— like giving a hug.

Habakkuk was one of God's prophets. He lived in a time that was very hard for the Jews.

Other nations had become powerful and they wanted to take the land away from God's people. It looked like that was going to happen.

God's people were really sad. Things looked bad.

But when everyone else was ready to throw up their hands and give in, Habakkuk said, "Hang on! God loves us. Hold on to believing in God.

"God is so great, God fills the whole world with beautiful, wonderful things. Look! They are all around us.

"Even when things look bad, we can still be glad...because God loves us. God will stay with us, no matter what."

Remember what Habakkuk the hugger says, "Even when things look bad, we can still be glad because God loves us!"

Let's have a celebration.

Help the children put on the simple hats and badges they've created. Use tape to fit paper hats and fix badges. Distribute the rhythm instruments.

Invite the children to march up and down an aisle of the church, playing their instruments and chanting, "When things look bad, we can still be glad."

Encourage church members to join in by repeating the chant and clapping.

When you return to the front of the church, gather the instruments and thank the children for joining in the celebration. Give each child two animal cookies, one for the child, and one for the child to share with someone as he or she returns to his or her seat.

Prayer

Holy God, you are the one who makes everything possible. Help us to remember that even when things are bad, we can be glad. Hug us, God, with your love. *Amen*.

Thank the children for joining you and invite them to return to their seats.

90

■ ■ ■ ■ ■

Zephaniah 3:14-20

"The Lord, the King of Israel, is with you; there is no reason now to be afraid." (Zephaniah 3:15b, *Today's English Version***)**

Summary

In this reading from the book of Zephaniah, the prophet praises God for rescuing Israel. In today's homily, children play a trust game and hear today's story.

Materials

Bible
several pictures of roller coasters
several adult volunteers

Homily

Invite the children to come forward and sit in a semicircle around you.

Begin the homily be discussing:
■ Have you ever been to an amusement park or seen one in a movie or on television?
■ What kind of rides do we find at an amusement park?
■ What is often the *biggest* ride at an amusement park?
■ That's right, a roller coaster. Who here has ridden a roller coaster?
　— What was riding a roller coaster like? a little bit scary?
　— If you haven't ridden a roller coaster, what do you imagine it would be like?
■ We can't bring a roller coaster into our church, but we can try something else that's a little bit scary—and calls us to trust.

Seat ten to fifteen children in a tight circle with their feet together. If you have fewer than ten children, invite other church members to fill out the circle. Ask the adult volunteers to stand around the circle, arms length from the center of the circle.

Note: Use the adults as "spotters" in case children need some help.

Explain the game:
■ One person stands in the center of the circle.
■ That person crosses his or her arms and holds him- or herself very stiff.
■ Those of you in the circle hold the center person tightly with your feet around his or her feet.
■ Put your hands up in the air toward the person and keep your arms straight.
■ The person in the center then falls toward the rest of you sitting in the circle. You'll catch the center person and pass him or her gently around the circle, almost like a big beach ball!
■ You don't have to push hard; all you have to do is support the person and pass him or her in another direction.

To recruit the first volunteer you could ask:
■ Who has lost a tooth recently? When?

Invite the latest tooth-loser to stand in the center of the circle. (Allow children to pass if they do not wish to participate.) When the child is in place, remind him or to cross arms over the chest and to *remain very stiff*, which is essential for the game.

Play the game. It may be a little scary at first—demanding trust—but fun once children get the hang of it.

If you have time, let another volunteer be in the center of the circle. When the game is over, thank the adult spotters and invite them to return to their seats.

Discuss:
- What did that feel like?
- What did you think before we actually tried the game?
- Did you think it would work? Why or why not?
- What do you think now?
- We all worked together. We built *trust*. The person in the center was always safe, even when it looked like he or she may be falling!

Hold your Bible open to the book of Zephaniah as you tell today's story:

Zephaniah was a prophet who lived in a time when things looked scary for God's people.

There had been war and famine, and prophets had warned the people that God wasn't happy because they didn't remember God's laws.

Those things made the people feel like they were falling down.

Zephaniah brought the people a message of hope. It was a message that made them feel lifted up again:

> **Rejoice! Be happy, Jerusalem.**
> **Your God will not let you fall.**

> **God will lift you up.**
> **There isn't any reason to be afraid.**

> **God is with you;**
> **you will succeed.**

> **God will be happy with you;**
> **you will be happy with God!**

> **God says, "Don't be afraid any more, my people;**
> **I will lift you up!"**

Say:
- When you feel like you're falling, look to people you trust to help you.
- Remember: God holds you safe.

Prayer

Holy God, your arms are strong. Hold us and keep us safe. Help us care for others by lifting them up and working together. *Amen.*

Thank the children for joining you and invite them to return to their seats.

Zechariah 9:9-12

"Rejoice, rejoice, people of Zion! Shout for joy, you people of Jerusalem! Look, your king is coming to you!" (Zechariah 9:9, *Today's English Version*)

Summary

In this reading from the book of Zechariah, the prophet sings a song of celebration because the great king has arrived. In today's homily, children hear the prophet's song, talk about looking forward to something and sing new words to a familiar tune.

Materials

Bible

Homily

Invite the children to come forward and sit in a semicircle around you.

Begin the homily by discussing:
■ Have you ever looked forward to something? What was it?
■ How did it feel to wait?
■ How did it feel when what you were waiting for finally happened?
■ Waiting for something that you want to have happen is called *anticipation*.
■ Today, we're going to hear a story about how one person imagined people would react when what they were waiting for finally happened.

Hold your Bible open to the book of Zechariah as you tell today's story:

Zechariah was a prophet who lived a long time ago in Jerusalem. He lived there after God's people had been conquered by other nations.

When God's people were free to go back to Jerusalem, Zechariah tried to encourage them to build the temple there again.

Zechariah remembered God's promises to take care of the people even when times were hard. He wanted the people to remember God's promises too.

Even his name helped: Zechariah's name means "God has remembered."

Zechariah sang a song to remind the people about God's promise to take care of them. It went like this:

> Rejoice, rejoice...shout for joy, Jerusalem;
> here comes your king!
> He rides on a donkey
> and comes into the city like a hero.
> This is God's promise:
> "I will bring peace to my people;
> I will bring peace to the world."

93

Discuss:

- Does this story sound familiar to you?
- Some people remember Zechariah's words on Palm Sunday.
- What is Palm Sunday? *(The Sunday marking the beginning of Holy Week. The day when Jesus rode into Jerusalem on a donkey.)*
- The Bible is full of stories that remind us that God's love is always with us. When we read the Bible, we find lots of things that are familiar.
- It's nice to find something we know and use it in a new way. It helps us remember both things!
- How many of us know a song called, "Yankee Doodle"?
- I have some new words I'd like to teach you to that tune. This will be our version of Zechariah's song!
- I'll sing a line, then you repeat it.
- When we get all the way through, we'll try to sing it again from start to finish.

Zechariah's Song

Be glad, O Zion, here he comes;
a donkey he is riding.
Bringing peace and happiness
and singing this glad tiding:

God is great and God is good;
God is our salvation.
God brings joy to every heart,
to each and every nation!

Prayer

Holy God, you bring us hope. Help us remember that you are always with us. Fill our heart with joy and peace. *Amen*.

Thank the children for joining you and invite them to return to their seats.